If I Could Just See Hope

By Darcie D. Sims

Big A & Company
Wenatchee, Washington

Illustrations by Jim Maus SM
Layout by Clarence Matney

Published by
Big A and Company
P.O. Box 4181
Wenatchee, WA 98807-4181

Distributed by Accord Aftercare Services
1941 Bishop Lane, Suite 202
Louisville, KY 40218-1927
(800) 346-3087

Library of Congress Number 96-84899
ISBN: 0-9618995-4-9

To my husband Tony and my daughter Allie
And to all my family and friends,
thanks for always being there.
We are each other's HOPE!

About the Author

Darcie D. Sims, Ph.D., CGC, CHT, is a bereaved parent, a nationally certified grief counselor, and a licensed psychotherapist and hypnotherapist. She is the author of *Why Are The Casseroles Always Tuna?*, *Footsteps Through The Valley*, *TouchStones*, *If I Could Just See Hope*, *Finding Your Way Through Grief* and *The Other Side Of Grief*. She is an internationally recognized speaker and Coping editor for *Bereavement* magazine. She served on the National Board of Directors for the Compassionate Friends for six years. Darcie currently serves on the National Catholic Ministry to the Bereaved Board of Trustees and also on the National Board of Directors for the Association for Death Education and Counseling. She co-chaired the World Gathering on Bereavement in 1991 and will again co-chair the 1996 World Gathering.

Darcie is affiliated with Accord Aftercare Services of Louisville, KY and runs her own grief management consulting business. She is a Fellow in the American Association of Grief Counselors and is also listed in *Who's Who In America*.

About the Artist

Jim Maus, the illustrator, has been a friend of the Sims family for many years. He is a Marinas Brother, currently Director of Counseling at Knoll Catholic High School in Fort Worth, Texas. He is also a member of the Team of Directors of Texas Catholic Boys Camp near Chervil, Texas. Jim illustrated *Am I Still A Sister?* and *Perceiver's New Lunch Box*, both by Alicia M. Sims (Big A & Company, publishing) as well as *A Place For Me: A Healing Journey For Grieving Kids 8-80* by Alicia and Darcie Sims (a relaxation tape produced by Tom Smith Co. Dallas, Texas). He designed the cover for the audio tape *If I Could Just See Hope* and is hard at work dreaming up other artist projects for Big A & Company Productions.

Acknowledgments

How do you say "Thank You" for believing in a dream? How do you say "Thanks" for keeping a light burning in the window, for keeping cookies in the jar and for teaching me about hope? Thank you isn't big enough, but a hug and love in endless supply to:

Andrea Gambill, editor, *Bereavement* magazine
Jim Maus, artist
Clarence Matney, layout and design
Sherry Williams, Accord Aftercare Services, president
and the entire staff of Big A and Company and
Accord Aftercare Services

And an extra special hug and thank you for Tony and Allie...the lights in my life!

Contents

Introduction

Once I lived the American Dream. But then, as it happened to you, and to me and to countless others, it all ended. For us, it ended with a single sigh as our 13 month old son, Austin Van, slipped away from his Mom and Dad and Big Sister. At peace after a lifelong battle with a malignant brain tumor, Austin took with him all our hopes and joys. The dream came to pieces and we were shattered. No longer the American Dream, it became the American Nightmare. We are BEREAVED.

The world seemed so dark and silent. No longer did life seem worth living. The sun grew cold and the music died. There were no happy sounds in our house any more and the sun cast only shadows of sadness. Joy had been buried one afternoon in late fall and winter came to reside in our hearts. Would we ever be happy again? Would the emptiness ever go away? Would I ever laugh or dream or sing again?

I was afraid...afraid to breathe, afraid to care, afraid to love. I feared for our sanity, our lives, our happiness. I did not know how long we could hold our breath, but I knew we would surely drown in despair before long. We discovered we were grieving, not only the death of a child, but the loss of close friendships, self-esteem and self-identity as well. We were so alone...left untouched by those around us who must have been afraid, too. Perhaps DEATH is "catching" or perhaps no one knew what to say to us. I didn't know what to hear either! But, as the months passed, it only grew darker and we began to wonder if we would ever know peace, joy or love again.

If I could just see HOPE. If I could just see a light — any light, anywhere. God — it's awfully dark sometimes. Where is that place where light and love come together? I can't remember anything — not his smell, his touch, his sound — his heart. Have I lost it all?

What does hope look like? Where is that place I once knew so well — that magical place where heart and mind are one...where the music never stops.

Will I ever know that space again?

Sometimes I think we lose the light because all we can envision is the darkness. All we can remember is that the light went out. The world grows dark and cold and hope seems an empty place.

If I could just see the light at the end of the tunnel. If I could just see the last dirty dish to be washed, the last bill to be paid, the last weed to be pulled. If I could just see HOPE, then I know I could go on.

If I could just see the light at the end of the tunnel, I'd know how far I have to go. If I knew where the end was, maybe I could find the begin-

ning...

OUR LOVED ONES HAVE DIED, BUT WE DID NOT LOSE THEM OR THE LOVE WE SHARE. THEY ARE STILL AND ALWAYS WILL BE A PART OF US. WE CANNOT LOSE THEIR LOVE.

But, sometimes we think we do. Sometimes we cannot remember the light. Sometimes, especially in the early months and even years of grief, all we can remember is the pain and horribleness of our loved one's death. Pain seems to overshadow EVERYTHING.

At first, all I could remember were the awful things. I kept track of all the things I didn't have any more and made mental lists of the things I would never know or experience.

I kept looking for the aisle marked HAPPINESS. I thought it was a place. I kept waiting for IT to get better and it only grew darker.

If I could just see HOPE. If I knew what to look for or how to act or feel...if only the pain would stop.

But we cannot erase this pain that is the price we pay for love. The pain of this darkness will always be with us. But it can change its intensity and its depth. It can change its color, but only with our own efforts. No one can make the journey for us. We must travel this path ourselves, but perhaps we do not have to go alone...

So, come with me in search of hope. Perhaps somewhere within these words will be the flicker of light that you've been seeking. Each piece is a vignette of grieving — a diary of sorts, sketching the journey through the SEASONS OF GRIEF. We are always in search of hope, in search of that magical moment when we REMEMBER FIRST THAT OUR LOVED ONE LIVED.

Hope isn't a place or a thing. HOPE is not the absence of pain or fear or sadness. HOPE is the possibility of renewed JOY...it's the memory of love given and received. Hope is here, within the magic and the memories of your heart.

Hope is US...you and me and the person next to you and across the room and down the street and in your dreams. WE ARE EACH OTHER'S HOPE.

Good-bye

Somewhere, sometime, somehow, it must get better. I believe that. It's just that I'm an impatient person and I want it to happen NOW. I don't want to face a new season with the same old feelings, the same old hurts, the hurts that seem unending.

September is a good-bye month: good-bye to the heat of summer (good riddance!) good-bye to sand in the shoes and melted popsicles. Good-bye to sunburn, mosquitoes and watermelon. Good-bye to fireflies, beach picnics and sweat. Good-bye to shorts, a bathing suit that didn't quite live up to its reputation of "one size fits all" and good-bye to bare feet.

There have been too many good-byes this time. I can't bear another single one. And yet, as the leaves begin their downward spiral, I know that good-bye has become a permanent part of life.

September is the month we pack away summer and turn our energies to gathering nuts for the long winter. We store away the sandals and the beach towels and begin the search of those things we so carefully packed away last spring when we were saying good-bye to winter. Is good-bye the only word we seem to know any more?

How come some people can say good-bye so easily while others (me, at least) have such a hard time with two syllable words? How come some people are saying good-bye to hurt and it seems like I'm just beginning? Does pain last forever or do some just learn to ignore it? Do some good-byes hurt less than others? Are some griefs less than others? Do good-byes always hurt?

Does good-bye come in "one size fits all?"

Do you hurt as much as I do, sometimes? Or is my grief bigger than yours?

I think it is.

I must hurt more than you do...my grief IS bigger. My grief will take longer and hurt more. I can wallow here a bit longer than you can because my good-bye was worse than yours...how do I know? I'm the one who is living it! I ought to know how much I hurt and I KNOW it's more than you! You see, my good-bye was worse than your BECAUSE...

BECAUSE...it's mine!

We play a strange game...we grieving people. A friend of mine called it "BEREAVEMENT ONE-UPMANSHIP." Funny how we humans like to compete — even in good-bying! We like to compare everything...even hurt. We listen to the pains of the world and then rate them according to our own personal scale...always placing our own pain at the top end of the measure.

My good-bye took a long time...yours only moments. My good-bye has a name...yours merely a dream. My good-bye was terrible...yours sounds less awful than mine...at least you didn't watch the suffering. At least you didn't hear the pain...at least...

My hurt is bigger than yours because there are few memories of goodness left...they have all been destroyed by the horror of the coming of the good-bye. I have nothing left but ugliness...my good-bye was worse than yours.

I hurt more than you do because...we each have a thousand reasons why our pain is more than any others. It is my pain and it is my hurt and I KNOW it is the worst of all. We even envy some of the good-byes we learn about... "At least you had a few moments to say good-bye," or "at least you knew what was happening"...or "at least he just left you. He didn't die."

"AT LEAST"...the words we put in front of your pain in order to measure ours.

Are there some good-byes that do hurt less than others? WE think so. But can that be true? Does pain know quality or only quantity? Can you measure pain scientifically and be absolutely certain that there are degree of hurt? The answer, I suppose, is yes, you can measure the quality and quantity of pain. BUT NOT MINE!

Is the sound of quiet any less because of the reasons behind the good-bye? Is the room just as empty, the heart just as wounded if the good-bye isn't just as ours? Does September arrive any sooner or stay longer if we have said farewell to someone?

We are all afraid at some point in our existence and for all of us, there is a first day at school...many, many times. Can we measure hurt and fear with the same numbers? Can we measure the sadness of the leaves as we measure the sadness of ourselves?

We try. And we fail. We think we can qualify hurt by circumstances. We think we can measure pain by degrees and relationships. We hope we can find Band-Aids big enough to protect our ouchies, sometimes not realizing the rest of the world may be hurting too.

We play the game well...this one-upmanship. Yet, we will never dis-

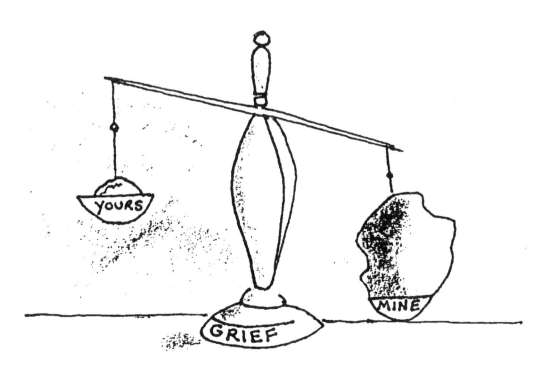

cover the other side of good-bye if we negate the depths of hurt that all the world knows.

Some do hurt more than others. Some pains are less than yours, but only if you don't own them. Your hurts and pains are yours and no one else can measure them for you. Nor can you measure any others'.

The only measure for pain and grief is that it is all too much. Whether September brings you an empty room for the first time or a new lifestyle to live or less money to spend or one less leg to stand on or a grave to decorate, good-bye is a painful process.

Maybe it's time for us to realize that any one's good-bye may be the most painful they have ever said…regardless of how it looks to us. Maybe, good-bye does mark the ending of some things. And endings often hurt…and most hurt is too much, if it belongs to you.

September…a good-bye to summer months. My hurts are no greater nor any less painful than yours…just as your sand castles hold dreams no smaller than mine. Grief is saying good-bye to the innocence of summer. And hurt is all too much for anyone to bear alone.

So maybe we can get through September together…you with your hurt and me, with mine. Maybe we can learn to hurt together, helping each other find the song of September…a time to remember…a time to gather in the summer memories and tuck them away for the winter. And save the sand from your shoes. It might come in handy later. No one ever said we couldn't have sand castles in the snow.

Guilt

Most of us have experienced guilt at some point in our lives. Sometime, somewhere, somehow, guilt has become a part of our awareness. Guilt, in fact, should be called the Number One Disease in America! We feel guilty about EVERYTHING. We feel guilty when we feel bad, when we are sick, tired or late. We feel guilty because it's only meatloaf. We eat because we are guilty and we starve ourselves for the same reasons. We give up ice cream because of guilt and pretend to "love" broccoli as much as cheesecake. We clean house, iron permanent-press shirts and call home because of guilt. We balance the checkbook, stop at traffic lights and watch the speedometer either because we already feel guilty or we think we should.

FAULT and BLAME are companions to guilt and seem to be interchangeable. It is always someone's fault. "Someone is to blame for this…" is probably one of the first complete sentences uttered by man (woman?!) when speech was invented. We are SO good at accepting blame and fault and guilt that we do it without even noticing. We apologize for the traffic jam. We feel badly about not eating enough fiber and we are convinced that if only something else had happened, then THIS would not have occurred.

IF ONLY…perhaps the two most difficult words to live with in the human experience. "If only I had known…", " If only I had listened…", "If only we had been there…", "If only we'd gone to the doctor sooner…" The IF ONLYS echo throughout history…each accompanied by the worst feeling of all…GUILT.

Guilt is such an overwhelming emotion. It colors our thinking, our actions, our reactions. We do things because we already are guilty or because we don't want to be guilty. We send cards, make phone calls, put off doing things and do other things that we really would like to put off…all because of GUILT.

The other side of guilt is responsibility. Who is responsible for THIS? What things do we KNOW we SHOULD HAVE changed? What pieces of the puzzle should we have played differently? IF ONLY and SHOULD HAVE become the mile markers on this journey. The more we look for them, the more IF ONLYS we find.

We revisit the events in our life a thousand times and then, again and again, searching for anything we could have done differently. Some little twist or turn that would have set the scene differently — that would have turned the ending ever so slightly. We agonize over the smallest details that we didn't see or forgot to do or ignored. We search the past for keys to the future we grieve for…our present and our future are because of our guilt…for we believe ourselves to be ultimately responsible for the events that have created our now.

Even if we can step outside ourselves for a moment and allow rational thinking to return, the secret, private inner conversations still search for IF ONLY…a desperate search for some reason, for some explanation of WHY. Surely SOMEONE is to BLAME for THEN and NOW! If no one else is available, we will accept the guilt ourselves and we begin to KNOW that our loved one died because of something we did or did not do, think, know or believe.

GUILT becomes one of the most difficult parts of the journey. It lingers perhaps far longer than any other emotion. There is always something we can rethink, replay, relive…In hopes of…in hopes of WHAT? IF ONLY is a sentence we never finish…because we know it isn't for a different ending. IF ONLY becomes the title of every thought we have.

If GUILT is the number one disease in America, then surely we must be on the verge of a cure! We can fix just about everything else. They have even discovered fat-free fat (although the fat-free ice cream does not rate the description of decadence!). We must be close to discovering a pill or potion or thought process that will alleviate the pangs of guilt that cling to the arterial walls and "gum up the works" within the heart and soul.

Until the cure is patented, I have a few tricks of my own that have weathered more than a few guilt trips. Whenever I feel overwhelmed with guilt, I write them down. I make FLASH CARDS of my guilts. Each guilt has its own card. I can shuffle these guilt cards to my heart's content, arranging and rearranging them according to my mood. I can list the guilts chronologically, according to the way things really happened (or should have happened). I can arrange them in order of importance or in order of pain still felt. I can manipulate those guilt cards until I begin to feel a sense of control. I can select one or two to carry with me, just in case I forget what I am feeling guilty about. And once in a great while, I can tear one up and throw it away.

I have also perfected the technique of catastrophizing. When I am really "into being guilty," I have learned to take my guilt to the very farthest limit possible. This works best on current guilts rather than on past guilts, but let me give you an example. Several months ago, I visited my sister for a family celebration. It was my job to put the turkey in the oven before joining the family across town. I spent a great deal of time figuring out how to turn on her fancy oven, complete with timers and remote controls. I then dashed out of the house, hoping not to be late. When we returned much later, we discovered that I had indeed, set the oven correctly and everything was working properly. I had, however, forgotten to put the turkey in the oven. Therefore, I ruined what was supposed to be a lovely dinner party. Of course, I had ruined everything by then…my nephew's graduation, my sister's dinner party (and reputation as a hostess), the joy of being together as a family…etc. etc. etc. It just got worse and worse until I remembered another guilt from a long time ago, and suddenly, a cold, uncooked turkey seemed a bit silly…

Grieving people seem to develop a new sense of what really matters…and cold turkey can hardly match the emptiness of the chair at the table. GUILT should be saved for the really BIG stuff.

When the REALLY BIG STUFF hits, there is only one thing to do. Pay attention! Don't deny the guilt that sweeps over you. Let it come, acknowledge it, experience it and then, LET IT GO. The only "cure" I know for our kind of guilt is to remember this: IF YOU COULD HAVE, YOU WOULD HAVE.

Trust yourself! You (and I) did everything possible at the moment. It wasn't enough or right or whatever…but we did what we were able to do, think and believe. If you had known what was going to happen in the future, you would have changed the present so you didn't have to live in the past. Trust that…believe it! GUILT is a human emotion and we must learn to forgive ourselves for making mistakes, for not hearing clues that

may not have been there, for not seeing what seems so clear NOW. We cannot go back and rewrite the script. We just have to learn to live with the guilt of being less than magicians, capable of foretelling the future.

There are no crystal balls or magic wands. Work at learning to forgive yourself for living. Only then can the music begin again. Take care of yourself, eat right (put a few chocolate chips in the oat bran), obey the speed limit, open the curtains and claim today. It is ours. In spite of our inability to manage it well, the day is ours. Use it to find not the one thing you could have changed, but to find the things that you can do NOW to recapture the love you haven't lost. Our loved ones have probably forgiven us...perhaps we should try that ourselves.

I'm counting on Heaven being guilt-free...at least they better have REAL ice cream!

Gifts

The holidays are coming! And most of us are not ready. I sometimes wonder if I will ever be ready again.

I tried making out my gift list today, but tears kept getting in the way. It's so HARD to think about gifts and fun when a loved one has died. What do I give to the family who is learning to live with an empty space at the table? What do I give to the hurting parent whose dreams are shattered? To the widow whose bed is empty? To the widower who hasn't mastered the microwave yet? What do I give to the siblings, the grandparents, the relatives, the friends, to all who are grieving the loss of someone special? What do I give myself?

What can we give to ourselves when we hurt so badly on days when the rest of the world seems so happy? What can we give to ourselves when signs tell us (in August!) that the holidays are coming and we feel we're not ever going to be ready again?

Gifts for the grieving can be difficult. But we must find something to wrap up and exchange with each other. We must not let death rob us of everything! Whether this is your first holiday season in THE VALLEY or you've been here a long time, you still need gifts. We each need something to unwrap, some surprise, some reminder that someone loves us enough to shop for us! If I could, I would give you:

PATIENCE. We are always in a hurry. We want things to be better NOW. We live in a world of OUGHTS and SHOULDS and suffer from guilt because we cannot meet our own expectations. I would give us all a hefty package of patience: patience with ourselves and with others and with the world in general. It may not be perfect. In fact, sometimes it is downright lousy. It's unfair, painful and awful. Patience might not cure the ills of the world, but I might be able to survive the turmoil if I had some tolerance of the imperfections of the human race. Patience is a hard gift to wrap, but one which we need.

TIME. Time is a funny gift. Some people never have enough while others seem to drown in endless hours. Time often becomes a painful yardstick against which we measure ourselves and each other. "Time heals all hurts" is an often heard phrase which falls short of healing anything. Yet, time is the only way to get from one day to another, from one moment to the next. Until we invent some magical transportation system to hurry the journey to togetherness, we'll just have to take it one moment at a time. It will not heal anything, but it might help soften the hurt and distance the pain. I will hurt the rest of my days, but time will change the intensity of that hurt.

MEMORY. When someone we love dies, memory seems more like a cruel attack rather than a gift. We cannot think of a single image that does not result in hurt. We cannot bear to look at pictures or to think of our loved ones...the pain is simply too great. Yet, even though we fear it, memory does not wither and die. It grows softer around the edges and if we allow it, memory can become our tie to the past and our bridge to the future. I would give you the gift of memory, for no matter how painful the memory may be, remember that you have it! If you had not loved at all, memory would be empty. Give yourself time and patience and learn to cherish the memories. Don't lose them in the fog of grief. Hold onto them tightly.

If you have but few memories of your loved one, then ask others to help you retrieve whatever memories they have of your loved one. Ask for pictures, stories, mementos of the life you love so dearly.

And if you have a memory of someone who has died, wrap it up and give it freely to those who are left behind. In sharing those memories is born the beginning of hope and healing.

PEACE. A most requested gift, often sought, many times not found. Perhaps because we are looking for someone to give it to us and peace is something that comes from within. My gift to you would be the strength to search for it and once found, the courage to allow it to live within you once again. Peace is that feeling of contentment that comes when the fighting is finished and the land is swept clean and flowers begin to bloom once again. Let the past remain where it is and nurture the seeds you plant today in hope of whatever lies ahead.

HOPE. We cannot live without hope, yet as we grieve, we often lose all sense of hope. We sink into hopelessness and despair and fear we may never feel happy or hopeful again. A gift of hope is most needed by those whose pain has robbed them of all feelings. I learned to honor the pain I felt because, at least, I felt something. Hope is a phone call, a note, a cupcake that says, "I'm here." This holiday, call someone you have thought about but not spoken to simply because you did not know what to say. Remember, it does not matter what you say as long as you say something! Your presence is a gift of hope.

PICTURE FRAME. Frame a beloved picture in a new frame. It will symbolize the blending of the past with the present and reflect a changed but still loved life-scape.

HUGS. Better than a new bathrobe and furry slippers! We miss the physical contact with our loved ones and a hug can ease the distance be-tween what was and what it is. Even those who do not like hugs can give and receive them verbally or visually. Hugs span the space between the heart and the soul and remind us that we are alive.

LOVE. Lost forever or so it seems. Without it, the world is colorless, the present bleak, the future hopeless. If I could, I'd wrap it in gold and silver and rainbow colors for you. I'd sing you all the songs you have stored in your heart and read all the lines of love written in your memory. But I cannot give you love you have not lost. I can only help you redis-cover it. Search for it, find it!

How do you search for love that has gone...that is buried deep within the ground or been cast to the winds? Where do you look when your eyes are too misty with tears to focus on anything except the pain? What store or catalog carries love? What I really want is my loved one back! In which aisle do I search for him? Where do you search for love?

You begin here...by understanding that love isn't something you toss out, bury, pack or forget. Love isn't something that ends with death. It's

Our Holiday list

may we have

- PATIENCE
- MORE TIME
- MEMORIES
- PEACE
- HOPE
- HUGS
- A NEW PICTURE FRAME!
  and...
  most of all....
  LOVE!!!

from ALL of US
To YOU

still here — just not in the package we expected.

We will not erase that pain...now or ever. The pain of these holidays will always be with us, but it will change its intensity and its depth. We can find the gifts our loved one gave us...

Make a list of the intangible gifts your loved one gave to you. Write down each one and then think of how you are going to share that gift with someone else. When you share one of the gifts your loved one gave to you, you are passing on the love you both shared.

Did you receive companionship? Then give the gift of company to someone who may know no other in the world. Did you receive the gift of JOY? Then find a way to spread that joy throughout the world. Did you receive the gift of funny stories or great cookies...then share them! It is in the giving that we receive...it is in the giving that we truly learn that love didn't die.

Write each of these "gifts" from your loved one on strips of paper and place these strips inside a small box. Wrap that box in the most beautiful holiday wrapping you can find. You may wish to place this gift box under your tree, or you might stash it under your pillow or in a secret place. But, wherever you place it, know it holds treasures far beyond our human capacity to understand. It holds tangible evidence that someone lived...that someone loved us enough to give us something! It is a re-minder that we did exchange gifts and that we still have those gifts, even if the giver has gone.

Begin to let the joy of your loved one's life take the place of the hurt and pain of his death. They LIVED...WE LOVED...WE STILL DO! May these holidays be wondrous for you. May you find the gifts of joy and remembrance that come with love given and received. These are the treasures of your life. May you rediscover them again and again.

Who Am I Now?

Why am I a thousand piece
…puzzle
When everyone else is
…already put together?

Why is the rest of the world
…a size 10?

Why does the grass grow greener
…next door?
B
E
C
A
U
S
E……I am a thousand
piece
puzzle

Who am I NOW? Who am I now that my loved one has died? Who am I now that I have survived the holiday season and find myself deep into the gloom of winter? Why do I feel so scattered? Why am I a thousand piece puzzle when everyone else is so put together?

Why does January seem so empty? Why do the seasons reflect my moods or do I take on the cast of the weather outside? Just as the world is stiff and frozen outside my window, I feel dead and scattered inside myself. WHO AM I NOW?

I managed to make it through the holiday season, although the hows of that feat are truly beyond my recollection. I can't even remember eating the holiday meals (I do, however, remember doing the dishes…again and again and again…next year we are eating OUT or on paper plates!). I managed to smile and even to find moments of peace and joy in those glittering days. But, here in the gloom of January, all I seem to see are the scattered pieces of my life…cast before me on the card table, waiting for me to pick them up and make the picture.

But, what picture do all these pieces form?

I used to think I knew. I used to know who I was and where I was going and how I was going to get there. But now, now in the chill of January, I can't even remember where the puzzle begins and I end.

I think I'm still grieving and that surprises me! It's been…(too long regardless of the time frame you insert) and I should be getting better. Why do I still ache from a sunburn I got years ago when we were together on the beach? Why is there still sand in my shoes and why does your name still stick in my throat? WHO AM I NOW that the memories grow cold in January's chill?

Am I still a mother if there is no child to tuck in at night? Am I still a dad if there is no one to loan the car keys to? Am I still a wife if there is no one to snuggle up to in my bed? Am I still a husband if there is no one waiting at home for me at the end of the day? Am I still a sister, a brother if there is no one to tease? Am I still a child if my parent has died? Am I still a human being, capable of loving and being loved if the one person I loved more than anything has become frozen in time? WHO AM I NOW that my loved one has died?

The gloom has permeated even my toes and my whole body seems icy. Why can't January be warm and gentle — especially after the struggle of the holidays? I need some sunshine, some warmth, some help in turning over the puzzle pieces and putting them back together…I need some spring.

But spring is a ways off and I must (somehow) get through these days.

Perhaps these few suggestions will help you find the pieces to your new puzzle:

❶ Identify specific feelings. Do not generalize. Try to figure out exactly what is bothering you. Look for the tiny grains of sand that are still hiding in the bottom of your shoes. Acknowledge them. Be honest with those feelings, whatever they are. If you're angry, be angry. If you're sad, be sad. Be specific in your sadness.

❷ Pick your worries. Focus on only one worry at a time. Give up being worried about being worried. Prioritize your worries. This helps combat feelings of being overwhelmed and you can decide which worries to keep and which to send to your: 1. mother 2. children 3. family 4. neighbor 5. enemy.

❸ Keep a picture or two of the sand castle where you can enjoy it every day. You may not decide to make a shrine out of your memories, but don't lose the joy that you had in making that marvelous moat! Keep the sand you found in the shoe — you just don't have to keep it there! That's what memories are for…a place to stash the important stuff that we NEED.

❹ Become as informed and as knowledgeable as possible about this new world in which you live. We fear what we don't know, what we can't see, what we can't touch. Read, listen, learn all you can about grief. It's not where you planned on being this winter, but it is where you are. Look around.

❺ Listen to EVERYONE. You will receive enough advice about how to do IT (grief) to sink a fleet of battleships. Be grateful…at least someone is talking with you! But, FOLLOW YOUR OWN MUSIC.

❻ Be kind to yourself. You survived the holiday season and now it is the beginning of another season, another way of living. Learn to forgive yourself for living.

❼ Set small goals first. Accomplish them. Then, set bigger goals. Try starting with getting the garbage out on the RIGHT day. Then, open the closet…the drawers…the heart. Try going out. The next time you might be able to get farther than the driveway. TAKE YOUR TIME. It's a long way to the beach. You'll get there again…someday.

❽ Remember that life requires effort on your part. Make friends with the vacuum, the checkbook and the car. Become determined to learn to remove the box before microwaving the dinner.

❾ Don't wait for happiness to find you again. Make it happen.

I know there are good things on the horizon. Winter can't last forever. If those things turn out to be less than what we hope, then we will simply have to make whatever we get into something livable. That perhaps is the secret to melting winter into spring: the challenge is to always carve out something beautiful from the icicle. There is joy in living…if we allow time in the winter to reassemble the thousand piece puzzle.

Normal Isn't Normal Anymore

Today I started to take down the tree and put away the holiday decorations. Yes, I know it's February, but after the effort of creating a new holiday routine in my life, it didn't seem right to simply discard it after a few short weeks. After all, creating a new way of looking at the holidays took a great deal of energy. I tried a new decorating scheme this year. We hung ALL the stockings—whether that person was with us or not. We played musical chairs so there were no empty seats at the table and we even changed tables — we ate out! Things were different this year, but different in a more positive way. So, after all of that emotional effort, it just seemed silly to pack it all away so soon.

So, the decorations have remained.

I just wish other things could stay easily…do you remember what your loved one's voice sounds like? The voice in my mind is beginning to fade. I can't hear the melody as clearly any more. Some of the pictures are beginning to fade as well. I can't always remember everything in the closet any more and I think I got carried away last spring cleaning and even tossed a few things. I can't remember.

What did he smell like? Even that secret shirt I saved no longer has his special scent. After that many years, I guess I'm lucky it doesn't have any smell…but it's harder for my memory to call up the special scent of him. I can't smell beyond the years anymore.

What did he feel like? My arms used to ache because they felt so empty. And then, later, I learned to wrap them around others and some of that warmth returned. Now, I still wrap my arms around people, but they feel like themselves…not like him. Have I lost his touch? Why don't other people feel like him anymore? I still remember his hands, but I used to see his fingers in other people's hands. Now I see that their fingers belong to their hands…not his.

I used to see his eyes sometimes…in the faces of others. I used to feel his gaze on my shoulder. I used to sense his breath on my neck. I used to "see" him just ahead of me in a crowd or across the street or grown older in another person's body. I sometimes waved at him across a room or talked with him aloud as I rode the bus (few people in my town ever ride the bus with me anymore).

I used to fill my grocery cart with his favorite foods and I even ate beets (only once) because HE loved them. I used to keep his favorite cookies around and I used to watch the clock every evening…waiting.

I used to wait a lot. And I used to cry a lot. I used to hurt A LOT, but then even that began to fade a little bit. As I began the holiday odyssey this year, I noticed that Halloween was kind of fun and Thanksgiving seemed less annoying (although I still spent time with a bunch of turkeys!). And even the BIG HOLIDAY wasn't nearly as bad as others have been…of course, that is probably because of all the changing we did this season. I imagine we can't go back to that restaurant ever again (how could I explain the musical chair routine — only other bereaved families would understand THAT one).

I used to hate Valentine's Day and Easter and spring and summer and the beginning of fall and the holiday season most of all. They only brought emptiness and renewed pain and despair. But, over the years, I learned to decorate with the holiday blues and then, this year, I realized that red and green (and pink for the flamingo) had returned to the color scheme and that the new ways of doing things that we developed were becoming routine. There was no questions about hanging what number of stockings…we hung them ALL!

I guess grieving, which had become a way of life, was beginning to change as well. Or maybe it is normal to have a roll of toilet paper at the dinner table (a box of tissues never used to be sufficient). Maybe it has become normal to play musical chairs at a restaurant — each family member trying to figure out where to sit, after so many years of knowing exactly who sat where. Maybe it has become normal to feel that bitter-sweet-

ness brush past my heart occasionally. Maybe we are learning to redefine normal!

Maybe there will be a Valentine for me this year and I can cherish it for what it IS...not ache for what it isn't. Maybe...I'll leave the tree up and just keep changing the decorations! Hearts for now, bunnies and eggs for later, tiny flags for summer...a yellow ribbon for safe return. Maybe I'll keep the flamingos in the yard ALL the time...not just holidays (I can hear the neighbors now).

Maybe every day is beginning to become a celebration of life, not a memory of death. Maybe I'm beginning to remember love first. Are you?

Fear

I imagine all living things fear something. Those with brains surely have multiple and complex fears, but I think that maybe, even amoebae have fear. It's such a universal emotion (now I know some smart person is going to argue that since amoebae don't have brains, they can't experience emotions, but no science is absolute and maybe, just maybe amoebae do have fear. At least they SHOULD fear 10th grade biology students!) Anyway, for those living organisms that have the capacity...fear seems to be rather universal (satisfied?)

We fear lots of things: death, disability, old age, responsibility, heart disease, cauliflower, things that go bump in the night, pain, cholesterol, crabgrass, getting a traffic ticket, missing our plane, being too short, too tall, too fat, too thin...too anything!

Some of our fears are perfectly logical and understandable. We may fear for our safety so we lock our doors, never walk alone in dark alleys and turn on lots of lights. We may fear for our health so we try to watch our diet, exercise and make sensible choices about living. Our fears may help us make decisions: how to invest our money, where to live, what kind of car to drive.

Some of our fears, however, are born in the imagination. They often appear to be irrational or "silly" to others. But, fear, whether based on reality or fantasy, is a powerful emotional and physical response to CHANGE.

Change, even positive change, can give birth to an unsettled or anxious feeling: the first day of school, the first day on a new job, graduation, the wedding night, the birth of a baby, moving...unemployment, divorce, homelessness, death...

Change, the process of hello and good-bye, is often greeted with a feeling of fear.

Our experience or lack of experience influences our fears. Fears come and go, sometime seemingly at random. They may sneak up on us, drenching us in sweat, sending the heart rate skyward, and giving rise to the old saying of "quaking in my boots." Some fears attack from the front, but even though we can "see it coming," our body and mind prepare to fight or flee. I was always ready to flee from Biology. I was probably more afraid of the amoebae than they were of me!

We understand those kinds of fears. We try to prepare ourselves with rational thinking, stress reduction techniques and appropriate planned actions. All of these things help reduce our sense of helplessness, which is the foundation of fear.

We fear most of all, the loss or lack of control. Even if we don't really have control, we like to think we do and when we lose that sense of control, fear rushes in.

Some are afraid of being injured, disabled or dying. Some are afraid of the dark. Some are afraid of the light. Some are afraid of living. We all fear uncertainty and the unknown.

We arm ourselves with weapons against enemies, candles against darkness, faith against the unknown. And just when we think we've got it conquered, fear comes again...invading even our memory.

We fear we will forget. We fear we won't be able to. We relive, again and again, the nightmares and celebrations in our lives, the events that are etched on our souls. We recall tears and smiles, taste and smell and pain and anger and love and fear.

No matter how long ago we grieved, it lies just below the surface, waiting for fear to awaken all the memories...

Some fears have changed. Some no longer exist, but others have taken their place. I try the relaxation techniques. I try the diversion tactics, but sometimes, in the silence of night or in the glare of day, fear comes home. And I know the world grieves our universal loss of innocence.

We cannot conquer fear. We can only hope to acknowledge it, respect it and live with it. We think of those who stand in the face of fear as being courageous. Yet, we all have courage. We are all courageous. Courage is simply a matter of acknowledging and feeling the fear and still going on, knowing that you are afraid.

I am afraid of many things, but 10th grade biology class (and the amoeba) don't bother me much anymore. I use a night light in the bathroom so that's taken care of and I've even pretty much figured out how to handle those old fears that come sneaking back into my grief sometimes.

But, it's this new yet very ancient fear that sets my "boots a' shaking". Once again, the world holds its breath in fear...of the unknown outcome of war, of the uncertainty of battle. Once again, we grieve for the uncertainty of our loved ones, an ancient fear yet new to every generation. We acknowledge it and continue on, just as every culture, every age of mankind has done before us. Courage to us all, to embrace the unknown, acknowledge the fear and not be consumed by it.

I keep the night light on, my whistle ready and a ribbon 'round the tree outside. We're all afraid, but together we'll endure...and live with the hope that someday, those 10th grade Biology students won't have to be afraid...of amoeba or of war.

Memories: What Used To Be...

I live in a small, old town where directions are given in terms of what used to be..."turn at the corner where the general store USED TO BE"..."Go two blocks past what USED TO BE old Lady Brown's place..." Those directions are pretty accurate if you have lived here all your life, but to those (few) of us who are "new" (anyone who has moved into town within this century) they only serve as a barrier. I don't have the memories of this place to help guide me through the twists and turns of NOW. And it often feels as though I will always be a stranger here...because my memory bank is empty.

I don't remember when the bayou used to wind past Front street and I can't imagine having to wait while a slow moving, but peaceful alligator crossed the highway (nothing more than a paved road!). I can't look at the steel and plastic of now and mourn for the return of the Spanish moss dripping from the oaks and for the smell of magnolias. I think corralling the swamp is a sign of progress...but then, I don't have the memories of hunting for opossum or 'coon or the memories of my first frog "gigging" or hauling in a crab net right off my front porch. My eyes see things differently because they do not have a history through which to focus.

My town is very resourceful in many ways and it gives rise to many a chuckle for us "outsiders". They recently closed the pink painted plumbing store and are now turning the building into a blue painted plumbing store. It looks the same on the outside and they only changed the letters on the sign out front as well as the paint job. But they left the drive-in window and the coffee counter is still in place...the scene of many an early morning gossip exchange. I wonder what they will exchange there now...maybe plumbing parts. It doesn't smell like a doughnut shop anymore but they left the extra "p" and the "e" on the end of the name so now it is a Plumbing Shoppe. It still sounds like the doughnut shop. And for the first time since I moved here, I do have a memory of what USED TO BE.

I sense a lot of sadness…progress didn't improve things this time! It had always been a doughnut shoppe although they didn't used to use the extra "P" and the "E" on the end. I imagine even that change caused some stirrings in this tiny place where all changes are noticed.

But the sadness goes deeper than the simple changing of a doughnut shoppe to a plumbing shoppe…there is a sadness here that rings true in my own heart as well and I am definitely NOT of the bayou clan. You see, the doughnut shoppe was started by a mother in this town many, many years ago and it became the focal point…a place to gather, to talk over the events of the early hours and to dream about going to the big city across the swamps and bayous. It was a slow, comfortable place…a home place and now it's only a plumbing store.

More than a few families had begun their histories in that doughnut shoppe. Young men met young women and then brought their children to have a Saturday morning doughnut and then their children became young men and women and the circle just kept getting bigger…the family ties stretching to include nearly half the town. It was a mother's place…a safe haven against the outside. It was, in a sense, the scrapbook of this town…a gathering of memories. And now it is only a place that USED TO BE.

How many places that USED TO BE do we each carry in our memories? How many people and events are catalogued in the heart spaces, ready to be recalled at any moment? Some of those memories are stored pretty far back, etched in NEON and continue to flash, flash, flash across the mind and heart and soul in a constant symphony…

Some memories are peaceful, some terrifying. The music one hears in the memory is sometimes faded, sometimes blazing…but we never forget the song…even if the words fail our lips.

We hear the sounds of words spoken in love, just as clearly as those spoken in anger. We hear the pain, the fear, the joy, the confusion, the emotions that color each event we have stored away in the mind's scrapbook. We may not be able to recall all the details of any one event, but we remember the feelings…the hugs, the slap, the warmth, the emptiness.

The mind may abandon the event, but the heart always remembers.

We remember the words we said, the ones we shouldn't have said, the ones we wish we had said, the hugs given, the ones never exchanged. We remember the smells of home, either wonderful or less than so…but we remember just the same. We remember events we can no longer clearly recall, but emotions betray the mind and the memory is still there…sometimes trapped and sometimes freed to return to us in full force.

We remember the meatloaf. We remember the cauliflower. We remember the wash on the line and the chore list and the gold stars I never quite managed to get. I remember the music of my mother's hands dancing across the piano. I remember the moving, the newness of every place, and how quickly my mother made it "home." I remember being tucked in at night and having to stand perfectly still while my mother marked the hem on another new outfit she made me…how I hated standing still, but how much I loved those outfits!

Memories are our treasures…even those which cause us pain have a place in who we are. We are the sum of everything has gone before us. We pass on our memories from one generation to another. We are the carriers of the torch, passed through stories, through songs, through touch. We pass on to those who will come after us, the joys and trials of living…of coping with whatever comes our way as best we can. We become another link in the chain of humanity, a memory trace from the very beginning to the very end. No one can remember it all, but we each have a small piece of the treasure to safe guard for the next heart to hear.

Whatever your memories are, cherish them. If they bring pain and grief, listen to them, learn from them, but do not abandon them. If they bring peace and comfort, listen to them. If they bring tears and confusion, listen to them as well. For whatever else memories bring, they bring the past to the present and we can carry them with us to the future in whatever way we choose. You can release the pain in your memories, but only if you will remember them. You can release the terror, the terribleness, but only if you allow them to simply come to light.

Then, and only then, can memory bring forth the knowledge that

someone indeed, did live. I cherish the memories of my mother, even though knowing all I have left are memories. I would not lose those gifts in exchange for less hurt right now. My pain tells me I LOVED and was LOVED. And I will choose to celebrate my mother's life...not mourn her death.

May this Mother's Day be a day of memory for you; I hope it will be a day of warmth and joy. But if the only memories you have bring tears and pain, then draw comfort from knowing that, if only for a single moment long ago, someone loved you enough to give you life. And that memory is you.

The doughnut shoppe is no more. But I imagine no one will allow its memory to fade. Now even I give directions in this town..."it's just past what USED TO BE the doughnut shoppe!"

Memory...cherish it...it is the threads of our fabric...our history. And if we know where we have been, we might be able to figure out where we are and where we are going.

Thanks, Mom, for the memories.

Grief Isn't A Summertime Song

June is a season of beginnings. School is out, summer begins. Graduation occurs, freedom begins. Weddings are held, marriage begins. June is also a season of endings. School ends, graduation closes the chapter of high school antics and freedom from responsibility. Weddings mark the ending of bachelorhood, the dating game, ready cash and freedom. June could probably be best described as the hello and good-bye month, for each hello has an accompanying good-bye and each good-bye opens a possibility of a new hello.

Families gather to celebrate the triumph of youth over studies and to witness the march of the newly wed down a flower strewn path (to the reception where the happy couple will enjoy their last "non-casserole meal" for many years to come). It is a month of remembering and for reawakening grief as we mark the celebrations of hello and good-bye by the number of empty chairs at the table, by the missing faces in the family picture.

We didn't expect to hurt in June. We thought IT would be "over" by then. Grief doesn't seem to fit as well in June (like the bathing suit we had last year). Grief is understandable and perhaps almost acceptable in the fall and winter months. We can wrap ourselves in woolly shirts and heavy sweaters and hide away in the winter. We can spend long hours turning the pages of the scrapbooks while the snows rage outside the window...reflecting the inner rage within. Even in spring, grief has a place...we brace ourselves to "begin anew" just as the tender leaves and blossoms speak of a renewing earth.

But by June, by the time we gather to celebrate the family's passage into summer, grief "should" be over. Grief has little place at the graduation ceremony. Grief seems "wrong" at the wedding table. Grief doesn't "fit" at the beach (where nothing fits as it should — except on those who have never tasted the sinful deliciousness of a chocolate bunny). Grief isn't a summertime song.

Grief doesn't belong on the playground. Its rhythms are all wrong for the gentle sounds of waves washing on the beach. It doesn't feel as good as the warm sand beneath our bare feet and a heavy heart has no place in the

garden. The smell of coffee and bacon frying over an open flame should not be accompanied by the memories of other campfires and other cooks. Summer should be a fun time, a free time...free of the burdens of grief.

The sounds of June should be those of carnivals, circuses, POMP and CIRCUMSTANCE played by the school band, the tinkle of the ice cream truck bell and the music of children laughing. The winds are warm and gentle, the air slightly moist and the only clouds are those high, fluffy ones that look like marshmallows. We lie on our backs in the grass and gaze at those clouds in June, seeing all sorts of wonderful shapes...do you remember those warm, easy days of cloud watching? June is the month for that...not for suddenly seeing a loved one's face etched in that skyward fluff. June is for skipping pebbles across the pond, not for seeing the reflection of tears in the water's ripples.

June is the month for camp, swimming holes, fishing trips and salads. It's the month for flying kites, mowing lawns and hanging wash on the line. It's the month for running barefoot and picking dandelions and watching beetles wander across the sidewalk. It's the month for pulling weeds and sitting under the tree in the backyard and daydreaming.

But for many of us, June seems to be a painful month...each glorious moment bringing renewed hurt and emptiness...each bird's song a reminder of someone not there to listen with us. Each blossoming flower an empty joy...no dandelion bouquets to be delivered or received...no footprints beside ours in the sand.

June is Father's Day, Flag Day, Graduation Day, Wedding Day, Hello Day and Good-bye Day...a card seller's dream month! June is 30 days of summer, filled with what should have been and what is no more...highlighted by buzzing bees and dazzling garden gifts. How can grief survive such a summer song? I sit in my rocking chair, tucked away in a corner of the porch and watch the water wash across the stones near the shoreline in June. And grief finds me. I run to my mountains, hiking to the remotest points...yet grief finds me. I listen to the playground music, lost in the songs of a son I no longer know. I bake cookies with a recipe I can no longer share with the cook...grief still finds me in June.

We mark the passage of time by the tides of those around us. We measure

moments by the events of others: baby's first step, first day of school, graduation, first job, marriage, promotions, moving, death. We may lose track of all time, yet we never forget THE DAY. And when thoughts of THAT DAY creep into our June time, we squirm and squiggle and feel out of sync with the rest of the world who has "gone fishing."

Grief has endured the winter with you…it has become a part of you. Not like an overcoat that you can shed when it gets too warm, but rather like a thread in your tapestry…a living part of who you are. We cannot get "over" grief…there are no seasons for grief. It is a part of who we are…but only a PART.

At first it consumed us…seemingly replacing ALL PARTS of us. It overtook all our thoughts and emotions, wiping clean the memory banks and leaving only pain in its path. But, as we have struggled through the months and years of this journey, grief has changed with us. We are different that we were BEFORE, not better, not stronger, not worse, not weaker...just DIFFERENT! But the seasons march on and soon it will be the heat of summer and then the sliding into fall and once again, we will drift into winter...always carrying our grief with us.

June is a month of memories and they flood us almost whimsically. Yet, it's when the day is gentle and the song is slow, that the heart is open and summer time flows even into the winter places in our beings. Grief is now a part of our hellos and good-byes. It always has been — we just didn't know it BEFORE. So, even though it doesn't feel quite right, bring your grief into June and into summer and let it live...recognizing it, addressing it and letting it go, cast in small pieces onto the waves and winds that clear the canvas every day in summer.

Grief isn't a summertime song...it is a lifetime song, but it doesn't have to be a sad song forever. Let it begin to become gentle in your memory...don't be so afraid that you will forget that you hold on too tightly to the pain. Just as you still remember those summer times of your youth, rest assured you will never forget the melody of the love you shared!

Come join me on the porch and swing a bit in the summer breeze...the memory winds come calling any time...even in the summer.

So You Think You're Going Crazy?

I thought I heard the grass growing today. I mowed just last week end and it shouldn't need cutting again, but...I heard it creeping up over the sidewalk this afternoon...

I know I heard the weeds in the garden chuckling at me as I sat on the deck this evening! Just as I sat down and began to let the tension of the day drain from my weary soul, THEY started snickering. It ruined the moment and I finally went inside...away from the smart-aleck weeds.

Then the dishes started in on me and I'll swear that the dust bunnies under the bed were hosting a class reunion! In fact, the entire house seemed to be chatting and laughing and enjoying the whole show. The television held nothing exciting and besides, it's hard to hear the actors when the smudges on the screen and the windows next to the set are screaming so loudly.

I finally gave up and went to bed. Bed has always seemed the safest place to be when the house and the yard (and the world) start in on me. I dragged my favorite "snuggly" out of the closet and covered myself with the sheet. At last...away from the conversations that seem to over run my mind! But then, the mattress smiled...and I HAD HAD IT!

Isn't there any place where a person can go and not be disturbed by LIVING THINGS? As I raced through the house, the sounds got louder and louder. The dryer reminded me that it needed emptying. The oven cried out to be cleaned (self-cleaning my eye!) The vacuum started gunning its engine and even the clock kept ticking, ticking, ticking...

I left the house and hid in the car...what could possibly speak to me there? (Never, never, never ask that kind of question!) When the voice from the glove compartment ask me to clean out the old gum wrappers and toss out the maps from 1956, I knew what my friends had been telling me for some time now was true. I AM going crazy and there is nothing I can do about it!

I first began to think about going crazy shortly after our son died. It seemed innocent enough at first. Just an occasional sound that came from his bedroom or a whiff of his scent would catch me by surprise. I didn't think much of it...in fact, I rather enjoyed those little reminders of him. But, after sharing my first encounter with HIM with a neighbor, I knew the rest of the world would think me daft. So, I quit telling other people about my little conversations and my little encounters. I just kept them to myself.

They weren't THAT special (except to me), but I thought I saw him once, on a playground about half a block away. By the time I reached the fence, however, he had become the little boy he really was and not my son. And once, in a store, I knew I heard him tell me to buy the Twinkies...I HEARD THAT! And I did (and I enjoyed every one of them!)

I found myself looking forward to these little encounters but never sharing them with ANYONE. And for quite some time, little reminders of our child flitted across my life...just often enough to keep me going. But then, after a number of months (or was it years...) the messages grew less and less noticeable. I think I was beginning to "get on with my life" (one of the all time favorite expressions of those who "understand"...) and I guess I didn't NEED to have the contacts.

But, I noticed that I still clung to little things...I kept his picture very close to me. We had moved several times by then and we no longer had any of his room furnishings or very many physical reminders of his presence in our life. We didn't refer to the extra bedroom as HIS and life settled into its usual circus pace. But...I still kept his blanket. I had wrapped it in tissue and placed it carefully in the cedar chest, to lie in state until his big sister would one day need it for her child. But, I kept getting it out and hugging it.

I never told anyone that. I was afraid to. But I thought I could smell him whenever I held that small piece of soft wool. I KNEW I could pretend for a little while. And I KNEW I was going crazy.

Everyone in our family managed to keep something secret for years after Big A died. His big sister kept his favorite stuffed bear VERY CLOSE to her pillow, but out of sight. I found it only after bringing the bulldozer in one afternoon in an attempt to locate the bed. Dad kept a small treasure tucked away in his drawer and carried it with him whenever he went off to play ARMY.

We discovered we were all going CRAZY when we asked a neighbor to look after the house while we were gone on a two week vacation. We

handed over the keys, a list of phone numbers in case of emergencies and the pictures of Big A. She looked at us with sympathy and caution...I remember telling her the house could burn down or the burglars could take everything, but those pictures... We finally put them in the safety deposit box. Everyone else in the world keeps important papers and jewels in their safes. We keep a few photographs...our only tangible link to what was.

We once discovered a widow friend of ours often wore her late husband's bathrobe (I sometimes wonder if my dad wears my mom's...but I don't dare ask). Many of us sleep with an extra pillow to hug during the night. We sometimes set a place at the table "by accident" or keep the pipe filled and the slippers in the closet. We are reluctant to rearrange THE ROOM or even to touch the things...and when we do manage to touch and clean and rearrange, we ALWAYS keep something for ourselves. It may not be much (to anyone else) but to us, that tiny secret something is the one link we have with the reality that someone we loved DID LIVE. Because, after awhile, we may begin to wonder if that life ever really did happen. We do seemingly strange things...little routines that we may not even realize are a part of our beings. We sit in the same place, regardless of how many are at the table. We keep a look-out "just in case"...knowing "just in case" will never REALLY come.

We treasure the objects of our loved ones more now than when they were alive. It becomes difficult to throw away anything they touched! And we think we are going crazy. The rest of the world KNOWS we are and most of us are reluctant to confirm that assumption.

However, as I discovered when the yard began to nag me, perhaps I really am crazy. Do I hear voices that aren't there...doesn't everyone hear the driver-in-the-next-car's thoughts? Can't you hear the phone ABOUT to ring — just as you get into the tub (or sit down on the potty?!)

Has my hearing become more sensitive? Am I more in tune or out of tune with the rest of the world? Or am I going crazy? Does it matter to anyone else that I still have our son's holiday place mat...tucked WAY DOWN below all the other tablecloths in the drawer? I can't...no, I don't want to toss it away. It's ours...it's our grief, our pain, our healing. And the rest of the world will just have to figure out how to live WITH our craziness or pretend to understand!

No one ever talks about these "unusual behaviors" or secrets. Few books tell us it's "normal" to hang on to tiny mementos of the past. But no one thinks it weird to keep the old high school yearbooks. No one thinks it's unusual to still have your wedding dress or a corsage or your first shoes (which may be bronzed and on top of the TV). No one thinks it's crazy to remember...so why do we, the grievers of the world suffer under the burden of fearing for our sanity?

Because...we think we SHOULD BE OVER IT BY NOW. And we SHOULD HAVE control over these things...we should have the grass mowed and the weeds pulled and the dust bunnies eliminated and the dryer emptied and the bills paid and the house clean and the meals nutritious, colorful and full of fiber. We SHOULD ourselves into insanity.

And that's when the grass begins to make sense.

I figure as long as the conversations I hear in my head don't lead me to tall bridges, sharp objects or dangerous encounters, I'll be OK. If those things begin to happen, then I do need to talk with someone besides the microwave. But, for most of us...being crazy is simply a matter of being in touch with ALL of our self...the outer reality that everyone sees (and assumes represents the inner us). And being in tune with the interior parts, the secret selves who may reside within...and not being afraid of who we are NOW.

The past is past...but only if we allow it to be. Sometimes we need to carry it with us. Sometimes we need to let it rest. Sometimes we can't figure out quite what we need and sometimes we don't even know how to know what it is we do need! But, that seems to be the "normal" state of the human race.

It isn't enough to say it's OK to be crazy...maybe for you, it's not OK. But for me, being crazy is simply a state of mind and I can change my mind any time I want... I am a WOMAN (sorry, guys!). I don't think we're really crazy in the medical sense until we don't realize we are.

But most of you reading this just think you are the only one who has ever heard the frozen Oreos calling your name in the middle of the night

(I answer!) or you are the ONLY ONE who still has the bathrobe or dreads trout season (Christmas is no big deal if your loved one was a fisherman…but the sight of a casting rod or the smell of a bait shop…) We ALL have our little secrets…sometimes kept secret even from ourselves.

I quit thinking of them as signs of abnormal behavior long ago and I've been happier ever since! Now, when I hear his sigh or get a quick glimpse of his smile in the sun, I just say a silent HI and keep pushing the lawn mower.

Just remember, love doesn't stop talking to us just because we don't have to do its laundry anymore!

School Supplies

I bought a BIG CHIEF tablet today. I really didn't have any reason to buy it. My daughter is in college and would probably die if I suggested she take notes on a BIG CHIEF tablet. And my son, who did die, probably doesn't need one either. (I have this magical view of heaven where notes and homework and dishes and laundry don't exist...). But, as I passed the aisle marked SCHOOL SUPPLIES, I suddenly WANTED a BIG CHIEF tablet and so, I turned down that aisle and journeyed backwards...to a time when we once bought school supplies.

I hadn't been down an aisle like that in years. But, as I fingered all the different colored folders and noticed that crayons no longer have simple names like red and green (now called rouge and forest...) I drifted. The memories returned. I found myself searching through the piles of notebooks for just the "right one". I must have gone through 20 lunch boxes before I found one that suited me...not too immature, but with enough space so a sandwich would not become a pancake before recess and of course, a sturdy thermos with the latest hero emblazoned on the outside.

The search took quite a long time and before I realized it, I had accumulated enough "stuff" so that I needed a basket. Funny...I had only come in to pick up some film and now I needed a basket.

The sight of the rows upon rows of new pencils filled me with that funny combination of anticipation and dread of the new school year. Do you remember that? Half excited about the new year and half sad that summer seemed over and the endless hours of evening were about to come to an abrupt end with something called HOMEWORK. Even a new eraser in the shape of a rocket couldn't eliminate that grief.

My lunch box was red...all good lunch boxes are red. It would contain some kind of sandwich from home...mostly bologna with catsup, a few chips or crackers, an apple, a thermos of milk or juice and maybe a note from MOM written on the napkin. I always peeked during the bus ride in the morning and by recess, the deals were made. Trading sandwiches is as old as we are (maybe older...Adam and Eve probably traded lunches, too). And if you were really clever, you could parlay half a sandwich into a Twinkie (my mother never allowed us to have Twinkies...we always got fruit. But, MOM...I LOVED Twinkies. Please forgive me.)

My daughter always wanted a bright yellow lunch box and she LOVED a new box of crayons almost as much as I did. We would buy 2 boxes...one for school and one for home. I never packed Twinkies in her lunch box either, but I knew she had learned the secret of trading...apples don't leave crumbs!

I had visions of the lunch boxes and crayons that our son would need too and that's when DAD got into the BEFORE SCHOOL SHOPPING SPREE game with us. His memories lead him to one of those black, workman's lunch boxes and pickles. He never has been a Twinkies fan, but he could trade with the best of them. He had dreams of passing that down to his children.

But years go by and eventually, one does not have to turn down that aisle any more or perhaps you never did (have you dropped out of school after kindergarten?!) And sometimes we try to avoid the stores late in summer when the aisles mark the change in season ("never mind that it is 102 outside...we must try on these wool sweaters or there won't be any left when we need them"...my mother's words still echo across my mind). We avoid those aisles because such simple things as the smell of new crayons makes a lump in the throat. The feel of new shoes brings back a flood of memories that is only equal to the flood of tears.

Will IT ever get better? Will we ever be able to march down whatever aisle we happen to turn into without fear of memory-overload? Will we ever be happy again? Will I ever be able to color again...without watching the tears pool on the paper?

After all these years, I am beginning to understand that the answers aren't written on a magical calendar somewhere. I used to think that if only enough time would pass...IT would diminish, get smaller, get better, disappear. If only I could work hard enough, the answer would be there. Just waiting for me to discover it. I did all the "right" things in my grief. I probably did all the "wrong" things too. Some things worked better or longer than others, but always, the little sense of pain just beneath the surface would follow me. I couldn't shake it.

I finally understood that little pain piece is a part of me. It will not go away, but I can manage it (when I feel like it!). Sometimes it manages me and I get swept away with hurt and pain and then even guilt and anger come rushing back into focus. Even after all these years, there are bits and pieces of all of those feelings left inside. At other times, other bits and pieces come floating back…the giggles, the warmth of his touch, the fragrance just after a bath…the feeling of a heartbeat so close to mine in an embrace.

It's all there…sometimes tangled and twisted and at other times, neatly organized and cataloged for reference whenever I need a "memory fix." We are like a new slate every day…washed clean with each new dawn, ready to write a new adventure to follow. Yet, unlike the clean blackboard (that is actually green…modern technology believes green is easier on the eyes than black…but whoever heard of it being called a greenboard?!), our chalkboard keeps the traces of yesterday in place. To be written over and over, but never truly erased.

The fabric of our lives is often torn and ripped, but it is mended with tiny stitches, (tiny challenges, tiny triumphs, tiny yeses!). It is made stronger because of the mends, not weakened by the holes. My chalkboard is filled with all the memories…the good, the bad and yes, the ugly (Clint Eastwood should now appear…). We DO NOT FORGET much of anything. It may not always be right at the surface, but no one forgets the feel of new shoes, the smell of new crayons, the taste of a fresh jar of paste (again, modern technology has robbed our children of the joy of sampling library paste…white glue simply does not have THE TASTE).

So, I turned down the aisle marked SCHOOL SUPPLIES and let myself travel backwards for a few minutes…knowing it might hurt. But now I have learned that it will hurt MORE if I do not allow myself the opportunity to hurt. When we try to block out or erase those memories we end up hurting even more…then we truly do lose something. There are many kinds of grief and many kinds of hurt. But the greatest of them would be the emptiness of not having any memories at all…

I bought a BIG CHIEF tablet today...mostly because I wanted it and I needed to treat myself (a low calorie, low fat, high fiber choice). I wanted to remind myself of my own childhood with its own measures of hurt, pain and sorrow. And its equal fill of mystery, joy and adventure. I bought the BIG CHIEF tablet to remind myself of my children's journeys...one still in the making and one cut too short. I thought I heard my mom's voice as I selected just the right one and I know I heard her chuckle when I put the red lunch box in my basket.

I'm starting a new season, too. I'll have to write my own note, but the words will come out of memory...the greatest grief and gift of all.

Trick or Treat?

I t was an ordinary day. Nothing special or extraordinary — just a day, another step in the endless succession of days. There were things to do, places to be, people to talk with, plans to dream about. I wasn't really even thinking much about IT. In fact, it can be days, even weeks in between tears now (how nice...I once KNEW I would NEVER stop crying). So, I was a bit surprised when I found myself slipping back into the past, back into the memories that I hadn't listened to in a long time.

Maybe it was the fall air. Perhaps it was the leaves rustling down the street or maybe it was just "one of those things"...a moment when the door between yesterday and today is left ajar and time becomes mingled and blurred. At first I was afraid, but gradually I relaxed and let myself drift through the memories, caught momentarily somewhere between fantasy and reality.

It all started in the store. I only had a "few things to pick up" but I went down that aisle anyway. I was drawn like a magnet to the rows and rows of costumes, masks and bags of candy. There were spiders and bats and ghosts and skeletons and candy corn and little round soft-center pumpkins. There were plastic noses to try on, clown wigs to wear and magic wands to wave. There were jars of face paint and weird colored hair spray and false teeth and "vampire blood" in a tube.

The aisles smelled like warm rubber and I remembered the kind-of-scary feeling of trying on one of those ugly face masks. I never wanted anyone to know I didn't like being inside that mask, but my friends thought it "looked wild" and so I splurged my allowance and bought it...so long ago, but today, my mind remembered that warm, rubbery smell. I slipped backwards into memory this afternoon as I tried on a mask

at the store.

The costume characters have changed a bit, but the dilemma of "who ya gonna be?" is still the same. I wasn't the only one wandering in those aisles today, but I was the tallest...the oldest...maybe even the loneliest. I shouldn't have gone down that aisle. I just had a "few things to get"...but I drifted over towards FANTASY LAND and I fell backwards into LONG AGO.

By the time I got home (with the mask hidden beneath the few sensible items I really did need), I was really gone. I hit the kitchen with a crazed look and found the cookies. I rummaged through the records until I found THE ONE and then I hauled out the scrapbook.

And it was Halloween all over again. And it was the first day of school and the first day of fall. It was pumpkin carving time and time to rake the leaves into piles and then…jump while no one was looking. It was football time and cold nights and heavy quilts and roaring fire time…and cozy time and time when lists didn't dictate.

Once again, through the scrapbook pages, it became GOOD TIME. Funny how time erases the rough edges of reality and we see less and less of the sharpness and more and more of the beauty. Our vision into the past isn't very accurate, but it is ours.

I could still feel the warm stickiness of the popcorn balls (now we aren't allowed to hand out homemade goodies. Spinach fiber bars or coupons for fake fat ice cream have replaced real happiness). I remembered the excitement of finding just the right pumpkin and the anguish of costume selection. My fingers could still feel the taffeta and nylon net of a lifetime of fairy princesses and royal naves.

I ran down the aisle marked YESTERDAY and I smelled the smells, tasted the tastes, ate a candy pumpkin and fingered the costumes required for a life I no longer live. I "tossed in the towel," "gave up the ghost," "fell off the wagon," and tore up the TO DO LIST. I tossed out the rules and let myself go.

I took off the mask and put on the rubbery one…the one with the scary face that looks a lot like me on the inside sometime. I donned the costume, selected my goody bag and flew through the neighborhood…searching for the children to whom I had once given treats.

I kept searching the faces, looking for THE ONE. I thought I saw THE FACE once. I KNOW I felt his breath on my cheek and I, once again, became the mother counting the minutes on the clock, waiting for his return. It was only the PTA carnival, but he was so young and the night was so dark.

The pages of the scrapbook carried me deep into the magic, reminding me of the adventures, the fun, the challenges. Captured on film, that life seemed so far away…almost as if that life belonged to someone else. Were those my hands, holding the birthday cake while the candles melted into the frosting? Were those his friends and those of his big sister—all dressed up in the characters of THEN? Who could tell…the disguises were so perfect…each one chosen to hide the identity of the person within.

Did we really live that life or was it all just a fantasy, a wish so strongly imagined, that dreams became true? After all, Halloween is supposed to be a mystical night when lots of unexplained things happen. Maybe none of those memories are real…sometimes I find myself thinking that…

But then, the pages of the scrapbook feel real beneath my fingers and the pictures in my heart were still there even after I close the pages of the book. So, it must have happened. You don't get memories by magic!

The first knock at the door broke the trance and I struggled to get up off the floor, my knees creaking with the reality of age. It used to be easier to sit on the floor…making costumes and building table tents and planning "Indian attacks."

But the knock on the door jarred me back to now and the bowl of treats waiting beside the door told me I had only been dreaming. There would be no familiar face at my door tonight…except in my memory.

But there would be costumes to admire and characters to guess and ohhs and ahhs to dispense, along with the individually wrapped candies (made with REAL chocolate, however…Halloween deserves real goodies). There would be the sights and sounds of another night of memory making for all the little ghosts and goblins who appear at my door. Somewhere someone would be waiting for each one to come home safely…to inspect the "bounty" and to dispense a few select pieces before bed time. Somewhere, someone would be gathering in a few memories to sustain them in the future.

I had had my time and so had he. Our time was forever captured in the scrapbook pages and my heart. I could taste them anytime I needed to. It could be Halloween any time I opened the book and wandered back into my memories. I knew I had not lost what was…it is a part of me and even after the sadness goes, the memories remain.

I traveled backwards…so I could remember the TREATS in life, not just the TRICKS. A good friend taught me that and today I remembered. Trick or TREAT? You decide.

I'm Not Ready Yet

We should know better by now. It shouldn't keep surprising us, but it does. No matter how hard we try, no matter what we do to prepare ourselves, it still happens. Year after year, generation after generation, it arrives without hesitation or delay. It stays too long and never lasts long enough. It is filled with anticipation and dread and we never learn enough and we know far too much.

It is greeted with great joy and heavy despair. And it is always announced by the universal cry of "I'M NOT READY YET..." The HOLIDAYS are coming and I haven't even cleaned up the fireworks from the 4th of July. I'm still unpacking boxes (we've moved...again!) and the calendar says its TIME for the annual migration of memories and the Great Stuff the TURKEY contest (the turkey won last year). Because we're in another new place, there will be the dilemma of where to put the tree and how do we explain to the company about that one empty stocking?

Nothing fits this year! I can't find the ornaments. The kitchen is too small for the turkey and the flamingos are going to freeze in the 20 below temperature. I haven't memorized my address and the grocery store is in the wrong place.

We'll have to figure out where to hang a wreathe and should we go electric this year in the yard? I'm busy knitting little sweaters for the flamingos left over from our life in the SWAMP and practicing with the snow shovel. I keep forgetting where I've hidden gifts I bought during the summer and nothing seems to fit in this place like it did in the last one!

We were comfortable in the last place...but then I forget that is what we said when we first moved there, too. We always seem to be more comfortable in the last place...at least we know where the memories are and where to put them and how to handle them. Here, here in this NEW PLACE, no one knows our "story". No one knows our history...it is as if we have NO PAST. It's easy to blend in, but not so easy to settle in...and THE HOLIDAYS ARE COMING AND I'M NOT READY YET!

I'M NOT READY YET...the universal cry of all living beings. I'm not ready yet for first grade, for crossing the street by myself, for sleep away camp, for junior high, for getting married, for getting a job, for having children, for burying someone I love. I'M NOT READY YET...for grieving, for handling the holidays, for stuffing a turkey, for finding a place for everything, for living where no one knows my story. I'M NOT READY YET for Thanksgiving, for Hanukkah, for Christmas, for New Year's, for Three King's Day or for blizzards or frozen pink flamingos.

I'M NOT READY for the annual flood of memories that always spill out as we unpack the stockings from their tissue wrapped nest. I'M NOT READY YET for the clutch of pain that still wraps my heart in grief as we place the ornaments on the tree. I'M NOT READY YET for opening the door to greet strangers who are fast becoming friends but who may never know the effort it has taken to be who I am now.

I'M NOT READY YET to be "normal" and take my place among the normal people of the world. We look normal. For the most part we act normal. (we do, however, have sweater-clad pink flamingos in the yard, holding our SEASON'S GREETINGS sign...) We are normal...except for OUR STORY and for the tears in our family fabric. But no one knows those tears any more and I don't think I'm ready not to have a past just yet. I don't think I'm ready for no one to remember our hurt, let alone the joy our loved ones gave to us.

I unpacked the silver today, intending to polish it and place it in the dining room so it would add its shimmer to the festive decorations. I wasn't ready for the flood of memories that came back as I traced my fingers over the delicately carved designs in the coffee pot, remembering my mother patiently teaching me how to polish good silver. I wasn't ready for the loneliness that swept over me as I placed the tea pot on the tray and suddenly wanted to call MOM and tell her I was, at last and again, home. She had taught me that silver always spoke of a comforting home...and now that I had found it and set it out, I wanted someone

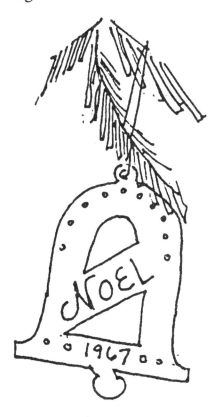

to remember with me all those talks my mom and I had shared.

I'M NOT READY YET to live only on the surface of life...I want to share my history with my new friends, yet it seems unfair of me to spoil their holiday season. It's not the same for me...there is still a lot of empty in my heart. Not as much as BEFORE, but now the emptiness comes from being too new anywhere to really belong.

So...I'll just have to figure out how to handle the holidays I'm never going to be ready for in places I may never be settled in. As long as we have the stockings up and the silver is polished and ready, then let the holidays come! We'll figure out how to tell enough of our history so we won't be lonely and so people will understand about the flamingos and the tiny empty chair and the joy that lights up our life when we grasp hands together in the family circle.

We'll decorate our new house (your new life?) with the treasures that speak of our history, finding joy in the memories they spark. We'll bring with us some of the old, add a few pieces of new and practice the art of blending yesterday with today in hopes of creating another memory for tomorrow.

I guess it doesn't matter if you have moved or have never left the same place for generations, it is still an unsettled feeling the first time no one remembers the journey you've been on. The first time no one mentions THE NAME starts a hollowness in our being that leaves us empty and feeling alone. It is as if the world has made its move again and everything that once was so awkward and out of place has now assumed a "normal" atmosphere and most of the world "forgets" the price we paid for this "near normal."

I'll hang the special ornaments, enjoy the silver tea pot and cherish the warmth of the love these gifts of remembrance bring. No one else has to know the story for me to acknowledge it and remember it. No one else has to know the pain for me to share the joy of having these things be a part of my **NOW**. We'll gather together and count our blessings, not only naming the ones around the table, but including those whose lives have touched ours in countless ways. One does not have to be present to be alive in the hearts of those who shared a few moments of the journey together. The heart never forgets…even when the world does.

No, nothing fits this year, just like nothing fit last year or the year before. But it's getting better, improving either with age or experience or patience. Or maybe it's because it is simply becoming a thread in the continuing fabric of our lives. We will probably always be a bit unsettled, unnerved when the roll call finds a name missing or a chair empty. But, then why shouldn't we be a little sad when a light goes out in our world?

So, this holiday season, gather in your blessings and count them ALL, knowing that no one else has to know about them for them to be real for you. Just because no one else knows THE STORY does not mean it is any less real. Count the blessings of the people in your story and find the peace that comes with counting a holiday of joy remembered and love shared.

Peace to us all…wherever we may be.

Winter's Gloom

I've packed away the few holiday decorations we got out and I've cried the tears that accompanied each treasured memory and piece. But, now what? I want to wrap myself with good feeling things again, to hide from the winter's gloom. Yet, it creeps inside me and lingers far longer than it should.

There is a letdown after the holidays. We're relieved that we survived the glittering season, but we are often left without a sense of direction or purpose when January sneaks up on us. There's the usual dilemma of what to do about New Year's resolutions (I simply have resolved not to resolve anymore!), and most of us are faced with an additional pound or two. They can be hidden beneath bulky sweaters until mid-April, but by then they may have turned into five to ten extra burdens.

Most parts of the country are cloaked in grayness; and after the holiday decorations have been packed away, the house seems emptier, quieter, lonelier than before. January also marks the beginning of the Great Gathering of Tax Information, the homecoming of the holidays bills and a long, dreary month of poor television. Most of us could probably just skip January altogether!

If you are somewhere in the valley, January brings its own special kind of pain. It's another year without...it's another year of memories growing dimmer. It's another year of discovering that grief takes too long.

In January, I grow especially weary of false hopes, too-bright smiles, plastic sentiments and people whose New Year's resolutions seems to be to cheer me up!

Maybe I don't want to be cheered up! Maybe I want to be depressed...maybe grayness suits my mood as well as my appearance! Maybe not, too. But what I do know is that whatever my mood in January,

it's MINE! And I want to keep it, thank you — at least for a little while.

So many people get upset because we might be depressed. They can't stand to see us glum! It's as if our emotional state is a direct result of their actions and an insult to their intentions. There are some real reasons for my gloom — some are weather-related, some are circumstance-related and some are just plain human-related. But it is MY depression, my gloom. They are my feelings and maybe I need to have them for awhile.

Depressed people are not fun. We don't sparkle at dinner parties. We don't radiate charm and warmth. We are not good conversationalists and we tend to eat more or less than we should. We are not the first choice for an evening's companionship and sometimes we stare at the television for long periods of time without really seeing the program or being able to follow a conversation. Sometimes, we seem distracted. Sometimes we can't concentrate and we forget who we are or where we put the car keys.

Sometimes we spend hours looking through scrapbooks and use inordinate amounts of tissue. But whatever else we may be, we are functioning through this situational depression. And although it looks (and feels) uncomfortable, a period of depression during the journey through grief is as normal and natural as the periods of anger, guilt, fear and hurt. It's just that depression is such a difficult emotional state and one that is hard to define and even harder to endure.

Grieving people often become the target for loving and concerned family and friends who simply cannot stand to see us "down." We become their mission. They become almost possessed with the task of lifting us up out of the gloom.

Sometimes, they hold team meetings (if they are professionals) or they gather in little groups to discuss the task at hand. We may become someone's project. We may even become someone's "New Year's Resolution." Plans are made — we must not be left alone. We must be cheered up, entertained, helped to "snap out of it." (IT, I suppose, is the black mood we seem to be experiencing.)

We're invited out to lunch, receive little "thinking of you" notes or plates of goodies (those ARE nice, but please don't stare while I gobble). All these efforts are attempts to lift us out of our mood.

We do appreciate those kind and loving gestures of concern. Please don't stop thinking of us or sending food or visiting! But, perhaps if we all understood that a certain amount of depression is appropriate, and maybe even necessary to the grief process, then perhaps we could all relax a bit about this mysterious emotional state.

Depression that is a part of the journey through the Valley of the Shadow of Death (otherwise known as GRIEF) is truly a natural and normal part of the process. One day, the grieving person realizes that even the pain of grief has disappeared. Where once there existed a searing pain somewhere near the heart, now there is NOTHING. Memories that used to bring tears and a tightness to the throat now don't even float past the mind. It is as if we have fallen into a vast NOTHINGNESS, a void where not only have the painful feelings left, but we have seemingly lost the good memories as well!

We begin to believe we have lost the sound of our loved one's voice, the special scent that spoke his name. We think we have lost the visual pictures we carry with us, and we cannot remember everything we once thought we knew about our loved one. Gone are not only the painful thoughts, but those thoughts that used to bring us comfort have left, too. We are cast into the gloom of emptiness...truly a most difficult part of grief!

Yet, I have learned that this vast emptiness is really quite a "busy" time for those of us who are struggling through grief. Though we may appear to be quite listless and may even "hibernate" for a time, this period of situational depression (as opposed to a clinical depression with accompanying chemical changes in the brain) has its purpose as clearly as do the other emotions of grief.

If we could think of this depressive "phase" or period as a **GATHERING TIME**, perhaps it would be easier to understand. When we tumble into the "nothingness" of grief, we really are busy searching for clues to the question, "WHO AM I NOW?"

When we have lost the framework of our personal identification, we must search for new identities and part of the grieving process is just such a search. Am I still a mother if there is no one to tuck in at night? Am I still a dad if there is no one to loan the car keys to? Am I still a husband or wife if there is no one sleeping in the other half of the bed? Am I still a sister, a brother, a friend...? WHO AM I NOW THAT MY LOVED ONE HAS DIED?

It is a painful yet necessary question and during this gloom that we seem to experience, we become busy picking up the scattered pieces of our self-identity and carefully turn each piece over, looking for the place in the puzzle where they belong. We are gathering in all the pieces and trying to create a new picture of ourselves, a new identity, a new "me."

It is an important and solitary job. No one can help us create the new identity we must find in order to continue our journey. We must each take the steps to seek out a new and different us — not necessarily a stronger or "better" person than we were, but definitely a different person than we were before our loved one died.

So, if in January, you begin to feel the weather's gloom creep inside you or you begin to notice a grieving friend's growing silence and a slowness to his walk, acknowledge the emotion and be gentle in your expectations. Don't dash over to help "lift" the depression. Instead, be supportive in the struggle to integrate the loss and redefine the identity of those left behind.

Depression that is a part of grief can become a more serious condition if not acknowledged, understood and addressed. If the depression seems to be totally debilitating or lasts far longer than even the grieving person is comfortable with, or it seems to include thoughts of self-destruction rather than self-identification, then further assistance may be required.

But first, explore the gloom and do not fear the absence of sunlight. Be patient with yourself and others, and remember that January may be the gathering time for you as you travel through grief. You can always turn on a light, get assistance, diet or turn over and sleep a little later.

Maybe January should be called the "snooze-button" month. Maybe a little extra kindness and patience will ease the transition from winter to spring. Maybe this "resting and gathering" phase will result in brighter blooms come spring. Maybe it's OK to wonder "who am I now?" and begin to search for new ways to answer.

January, the month of long nights, short days, little light and lots of time to think.

Don't lose hope just because the days are too short and the winter is too long. Snuggle deep into a warm quilt, grab a bowl of air-popped popcorn (for the health conscious) and spend some time with yourself. Invite others in when you wish, but only to share your journey with you — not do it for you!

See you in the spring when we will have to begin a self-improvement program to get rid of the extra ten pounds that winter causes, but we'll worry about that next month!

Cleaning The Closet

The lace has grown yellow with age. The edges are tattered and the glue that held the pieces together has long dried up, only a slight stain on the faded red paper. It is much smaller than I remember. Perhaps time has caused it to shrink. It seems so fragile, resting here in my palm.

The words have nearly faded and even the heavy crayon marks have lost their luster over the years. There's a smudge of unknown origin on the back, near where the paper was rubbed dangerously thin by uncounted erasure marks. The name is barely legible, the pencil lines so weak that only the mind can read the letters.

I found it the other day, while doing one of those winter chores: cleaning closets. It's nearly 25 below zero outside and it seemed like a good idea to clear away some of the trappings of a thousand years. February is the middle of winter month and most of us have fewer choices in this month than in any other. For us here in the GREAT NORTH, it is either shovel the walk or clean the closets. It's warmer in the closet (although not by much!) So, armed with dust rag, trash bag and the radio, I opened the door and slipped in…not really thinking about what I might find. I thought I was just going to clean the closet.

But, that first box sent me spinning. I found things I hadn't even remembered I'd lost! I finally found the holiday gift I bought for my sister last year and then so (carefully) hid away. I found snow boots and sand pails, a beach towel, three old paperbacks, a pile of magazines (all saved because I wanted to clip something "important"). I found shoelaces for shoes no longer "alive" and several things that had once been alive. I found half a chocolate covered cherry and part of a deck of playing cards. It was quite a treasure box — filled with junk that once had had some meaning to someone, maybe even me.

I sorted through the coats and clothes, painfully aware that "some-day" would probably not arrive in my lifetime — the too short hemline and the too small waist would not be mine again. I packed those things away, mindless of the hours and the drifting snow outside the window.

When I found the box of scrapbooks, I sat down...now that the closet had some actual floor space. I touched the bindings, not quite sure I

possessed the courage required to open the pages. The phone rang and forced me away from that decision. I left the closet and did not return until now.

That's when I found the old paper Valentine, tucked away between the pages of a life long ago. As I held that once sticky, but now only stained piece of construction paper, I felt a connection with other Valentines, in other lifetimes. I heard a whisper of another voice: my own mother's exclamation over my offered gift. It blended then with my voice, speaking across the generations of children bringing home paper messages of love. OH! I had forgotten THAT...it had become lost in the pain of memories.

It was a peaceful hour in that closet, listening to the sounds of my life, lived long ago and now remembered through the pages of these scrapbooks. I heard my own laughter and that of my friends, joining the laughter of my own children, seeking the laughter of tomorrow's bearers of paper hearts. Time does pass on...generations of hearts have been delivered and received. Generations of love have been shared just as generations of hurt have been endured. It felt timeless in the closet...as if when I opened the door, the giver of this Valentine would still be waiting.

Perhaps that is exactly what is happening...perhaps the engineers of all of our hurts and happiness are still waiting...waiting for us to claim that love and bring their light back into being. There were so many years when I could not bear this exchanging of paper hearts! There were so many years when I counted FIRST what I was missing...never realizing that in the measuring of my losses, I was truly losing what I did have!

The snow has drifted deep across the yard: only the tips of my flamingos' knit-capped covered heads are visible in the white. But my vision has been cleared somewhat this afternoon...by a visit in the closet where I found a memory that no length of time could fade. The lace IS faded, the edges tattered, but the heart always remembers and through the tears, the sounds of love given and received echo back to me.

I shall not waste another moment, living in the sadness that has permeated even my bones. I cannot remain in the closet forever...just as the snow WILL melt someday, so too shall this pain. And then, it will be spring and this little paper heart will bloom again…because I will make room for love to grow once more.

So, now this little paper message from both my past and my future sits on my dresser, reminding me each morning to make room for the happy memories as well as the hard ones. I had "lost" that Valentine from so long ago, but the bearer of that most precious gift of love has NOT been lost to me. Our loved ones DIE, but the love we share between us can NEVER BE DESTROYED. Love continues past all change and becomes the memory trace that guides the human spirit. Love isn't enough, but without it, the world grows cold and frozen…and the sidewalks never get shoveled and the closets never get cleaned…and memories get lost in the confusion of pain not healing.

Go find a Valentine…clean a closet, rummage through a drawer, search for some tangible evidence that, indeed your loved DID LIVE…and what a sweet treat that will be! Hearts and hugs to you this month.

Will It Ever Be Spring?

Do you ever wonder if IT is ever going to end? The calendar says it is SPRING now and still IT remains. The days are growing longer; the dawn arrives a little earlier and the twilight lingers a few extra minutes each week. The air moves in a breeze instead of a winter gale, but IT remains.

There are definite signs of a warming trend on the television weather map and I thought I saw a tender bud beginning to rise on one of the bushes. Some of the sounds of SPRING are beginning to return to the land that has remained frozen and barren for so long and yet, IT remains. The arrival of a gentler season is proclaimed by the seed catalogues that stuff the mailbox on a daily basis. But, IT remains.

The calendar tells me that Easter is "late this year"…is that because the Easter Bunny is getting older and therefore, a bit slower in his old age? The calendar also tells me that two months have already been spent out of the new year and "time's a wastin'". According to the fashion magazines and the store displays, we all missed spring last winter…why are they always a season ahead? Who wants to think about bikinis when one is bundled in sweaters 3 layers deep? Is the entire world out of sync or just me?

SPRING seems far away right now. There isn't much lightness to my step or to my heart and I figure my tulip bulbs got put in upside-down anyway (is someone in CHINA enjoying my emerging bulbs?)

The ground is still frozen up here in the far north country and the only thing peeking out of the ground is more snow. Now I know why Easter eggs are colored…it's the only way the kids can locate them in the snowdrifts. Never mind new Easter shoes or a new bonnet…we're still wearing parkas and snow boots. The traditional Easter Parade is really a march of the snow plows. Yes…the calendar may say SPRING is coming, but IT remains and I am beginning to wonder when IT will go away.

IT, of course, means SNOW, but it also means the chill of grief that continues to reside in the heart places and in the memory. We keep hoping that, someday, IT will disappear (the natives tell me that June is nice up here) and we keep waiting for the ice to melt. We keep waiting for the sadness to leave, perhaps just fading away one night as we sleep. But, grief, like snow and ice, doesn't simply melt away.

We thaw a bit and then an icy wind blows back a painful memory and winter returns. A warm breeze signals a return of gentler times, only to be blasted away by a whiff of perfume, the snatch of a song, a fleeting glimpse of a familiar face. It can be years later and STILL we get "caught" by a moment's memory and the icy winds of winter dash back in to take up residence.

We sprinkle salt on the ice, hoping it will keep the sidewalks CLEAR, but then it melts and puddles, only to refreeze when darkness sweeps across the daylight. Grief is that way too. We think we are beginning to thaw, only to be reminded, again and again, of our losses. The beginning of SPRING causes most of the world to celebrate, but sometimes, IT is too loud for us to hear the robin's first spring song.

We keep hoping for the MAGIC that will erase the hurt and melt the ice that remains at the core of our being. We keep hoping for a good weather report so we can plant the spring crops and feel the sun warming the earth. We keep hoping for the good feelings to return…we keep waiting for the US we knew to come back…for the night to disappear and the nightmare to end.

Waiting and hoping won't make IT fade away. Waiting and hoping are passive pursuits…a bit like buying the snow shovel and leaning it against the garage door. The snow doesn't get moved unless WE do it! It will snow anywhere it wants to…regardless of how much we shake our fists or sigh or cry! The winter comes and stays and stays and stays and IT can take up permanent residence if you let it.

But waiting and hoping won't re-warm the earth. Shoveling snow warms the body and keeps us limber…in preparation for the return of spring. Reading seed catalogues won't get the seeds planted, but it does keep the mind busy and the dreaming spaces in the heart alive.

Grief is WORK, not merely marking the passing of time. Shoveling snow and dyeing Easter eggs and planning the garden are WORK, too. And time seems to move faster when we are. Waiting for IT to melt doesn't seem to have much effect. But, facing the snow with a determined shovel, planning the garden with a hopeful eye and living THROUGH the winter storms of grief all seem to lead us to the spring season…where memory becomes softer and we begin to understand we, too, are someone new.

The calendar says its SPRING and so it is. If IT remains in your heart, take care and nurture yourself as gently as you water the tender earth. If there is still snow on your spring parade, wear boots instead of sandals and

remember you are not alone. Somewhere, some place, someone else is also struggling to make sense out of the rhythms of life. We don't have to know WHY in order to ask HOW...how to shovel snow, how to dye eggs, how to plant seeds, how to live with the empty spaces...just know you have to SEARCH for the answers yourself. They won't come to you in the magic of wishes, but they can come...if only you will look.

SPRING TIME...we cannot fill up the empty spaces left by loved ones no longer within hug's reach, but the snow begins to melt when we realize that love creates new spaces in the heart and expands the spirit and deepens the joy of simply being alive. LOOK FOR the spring...demand it for yourself! Let some of the ice go...find some of the happiness that your loved one brought to your life and let that light warm the seeds of healing. Your loved one brought LIGHT to your life...don't lose that in the continued winter of despair.

Waiting and hoping aren't enough. Grief is WORK, but the earth is softer and the shoveling is easier.

Advice

I miss my mom. I miss her words of wisdom. "A vacuum cleaner is not an appropriate Mother's Day gift." "A LADY NEVER walks with a cigarette in her mouth." "Don't forget your sweater..." "Hang up your coat, dear." "Too many casseroles aren't good for a husband." "You can make anything taste good if you have a good cream sauce..." "Smooth gravy takes patience!"

ADVICE. What to do. What not to do. How to think. How NOT to think. The OUGHTS and SHOULDS of life...the rules of conduct that are meant to guide us through the trials and the tribulations. ADVICE. A mother's gift to the next generation.

My mother taught me how to dust, clean the bathtub and make gravy without lumps. She taught me how to separate clothes BEFORE washing them and the importance of matching socks. She gave me a lifetime's worth of knowledge about cooking, cleaning and men, but she never gave me a clue as to how to live without her. She left me with socks to mend and the skill to do it. I use her thimble and the stitches just seem to know where to go. I use her cookbooks and her wire whisk and the gravy turns out right and I still fold the sheets her way...but it doesn't help the emptiness on Mother's Day.

I wear her jewelry and feel close to her. I named our daughter after her and smile as I dust the owl collection she loved so much. I hear her voice, guiding, advising, teaching me as I polish over and over again the intricate scrolls on the silver service. I see her gentle smile reflected in the wine glasses as I set the table and I still hate to iron the linen tablecloth just before Sunday supper.

ADVICE...words our mothers gave us in hopes of creating a better person, place or world. "Don't chew with your mouth open..." "Don't swallow that gum…" "Don't hit your sister!" "Beds are for sleeping, not for bouncing…"

Can you still hear the words? Do they still float back to you sometimes…catching you off guard and transforming the simplest of tasks into grief work? Why can't I put away the dishes without remembering the stories that belong to the gravy boat? Why does that little crystal bowl still make me cry? Why do I still put a few grains of rice in the salt shaker ("for moisture control") and why do I worry about the direction of the toilet paper roll ("it goes OVER so you can see the design").

ADVICE…words our mothers spoke to us in order to civilize us. "Don't forget to wipe your feet…" "Please shut the door — this isn't a BARN, you know…" "Don't spit at the table…" "You look so NICE in that dress (it was pink and had a BIG collar and I didn't look NICE!). "You really should have at least one dress…you can't live in jeans and sweat shirts all your life…"

My mother handed out advice quite freely, but always with the best of intentions and the kindest of spirit. Often her advice came at the exact moment I really NEEDED it and just as often, at the exact moment I didn't WANT IT! She KNEW me better than I knew myself and her few words were always chosen to help, not hurt. But I didn't always realize that at the time.

ADVICE…words that create boundaries around one's world. "You may not go in the street" and "Be in before 10." I lived in a world of matched socks, ironed pillowcases, full cookie jars, two working parents and a sister with whom I was not allowed to exchange physical blows. I knew the rules and what was expected of me (although I did not always abide by those rules and I probably never fulfilled those expectations). We always had food on the table and a roof over our heads. Some of our fantasies were left unanswered, but our needs were always met. We often thought we suffered but we never lacked for ADVICE…words of wisdom that had been passed down from generation to generation. Some of the words I grew up with had more than likely come over on the Mayflower!

I learned early on to work hard, chew with my mouth closed, carry a handkerchief and two quarters and wear clean underwear every day. My mother's advice guided me through childhood, adolescence, young adulthood and into what is politely called MIDDLE AGE. She prepared me well for coping with just about everything, including stopped-up sinks, a colicky baby, flat tires, lumpy gravy and power failures just before the boss arrives. She prepared me well for the crisis in life and taught me that while vacuum cleaners and appliances should NOT be considered GIFTS, one must be able to receive them graciously and treasure them for the love they represent.

My mother taught me so much…just as yours did. Mothers have so much to give and much of it comes in the form of ADVICE. ADVICE will probably be the last echo on earth and perhaps there is even a bit of AD-

VICE floating somewhere in space at this very moment. Even if you never knew your mother, she left you with ADVICE. DON'T is a mother's favorite word and it is often the beginning of her legacy to us.

ALL of us have a mother. Some have wonderful memories, some have few, some have none at all. Some are lucky enough to still have their moms attached to their memories and some may even be receiving ADVICE at this very moment. But, regardless of your status with your mom…remember that ADVICE was born centuries ago when LOVE was invented and given words. And ADVICE is our heritage.

"Don't" may be the most popular advice, but "I LOVE YOU" is the nicest. I learned a lot from you, MOM. If only you could have left me some words for now…some little hint as to what to do when the world is empty of your voice and I can't remember how to de-lump the gravy. I'll figure out the gravy…but I could use some help with the missing you part.

ADVICE…appliances are NOT suitable love gifts, but I'll remember the love that goes with it and be glad. Mom…I've got on clean underwear, the checkbook balances, the kids are OK, I changed the shelf paper and if we still ate gravy, it's lump free! Thanks.

Hasta La Vista

The wind blew today and I left the northern prairie. The fields were new with crops, the sky that too big blue and the clouds a fluffy white and the tears left a streak of dust across my cheek. The wind blew today and I left.

I hadn't planned on leaving (does any one?) so soon, but life doesn't seem to consult us at every turn and so, I packed up the teepee and followed the wind...wherever it will take us now.

I've got a sandwich, an apple, the house plants, the photo albums, the scrapbooks and a map. The covered wagon is packed, each life treasure carefully sealed against the transition from yesterday to tomorrow. I tried to pick out just the "stuff" we would need along the trail, but I think we took too much...but if the truth were told, we left too much behind. I wonder how the pioneer women did it...carting everything they deemed precious in life in a wooden wagon...leaving behind everything they deemed precious in life...following a dream that might lead nowhere.

The wind blew today and I left. Part of me is excited, part of me is sad. Most of me is tired. It's hard work saying hello and good-bye at the same time. It's hard work trying to separate the feelings.

It's hard work trying to get everything everyone MUST HAVE into little boxes with labels on them. It's as if we are trying to pack up everything that has ever happened to us and take it with us...the first grade finger painting, the pet rock, the first corsage, the sympathy cards, the graduation announcements and the stuffed animals that served as surrogate family along the way. I've got boxes of books, dishes, knickknacks and memories.

There's the miniature windmill from West Texas, the Indian rugs from the Southwest, the Mardi Gras beads and Rubie, our 25 pound green cement alligator from our home in the swamp. There are boxes of records left over from college days and stacks of year books, scrapbooks and boxes of photos as yet unsorted. There are clothes for every season in every part of the country and for every size we've all been and perhaps hope to be again!

There's a box marked AUSTIN and the tape hasn't been broken in several moves…it contains our share of yesterdays that I cannot open just yet. There are many boxes in our lives. There have been many good-byes. There's a box of mementos from every place we've ever lived which gives our house a truly eclectic decorating look. I am personally very fond of the pink flamingos, the neon EAT sign and our collection of personality bears.

It's hard to say good-bye to places you have loved, even if you have only lived there a little while. It's easier to shout "I'M OUTTA HERE" to those few places where the person and the place just didn't quite match, but on the whole, I'm more often looking sadly in the rear view mirror as the place we once called home fades into yesterday.

The trouble with good-bying is you never get to see the results of your hellos. I wonder what the landscaping in San Antonio looks like now. I wonder how the neighborhood in Abilene has changed. Did our grass come up in Kansas City? Did the dock sink in New Orleans? Did the new owners find the secret blueberry patch in the backyard in Northern Michigan? Did they ever build that mall in California? Does anyone remember the grave in Colorado?

Does anyone remember that we've been here?

Can you leave footprints someplace or does the wind always sweep the earth clean, erasing whatever traces of YOU have been laid down? Can one person make a difference someplace? Do seeds come up after they have been planted? I've never known that…I've planted many a seed, but have never stayed for the harvest…not once! I've enjoyed my share of someone else's planting, but never my own…did anything we've ever done stay real?

The wind blew today and it was time to go. It's always time to go in our life…hello and good-bye are words that come easily and are spoken often. But, sometimes, the good-bying part is harder than I expected. Like now…as the northern prairie flatness gives way to the rolling river hills,

soon to stretch into the mightiness of the mountains, is there a single footprint left somewhere on that prairie that I could call my own? Did I make a difference somewhere along the way? Did someone like my chocolate chip cookies or my freshly mown lawn or my pink flamingos in the bushes?

Did someone notice our frustrations as we tried to find our way in another new town? Did anyone notice our out-of-state license plates? Did anyone feel my sense of victory when I managed to find the grocery store on the FIRST TRY? Did anyone notice my quizzical look when I first encountered some of the unusual local customs? Or is everyone so busy with their own hellos and good-byes that we rarely notice anyone else's struggles with those two little words?

Two simple little words that can screw up EVERYTHING! Hello and good-bye...adventure, pain, excitement and sadness all rolled into one moment that cannot be separated neatly into stages, phases or emotions. We like to think we can compartmentalize, label and address each piece of the process, but in the end, every journey has both a beginning and an ending. And somewhere in the middle the good-bye becomes hello and I start looking forward instead of gazing back. Somewhere in the middle of change, the tear turn to twinkle and the adventure begins all over again.

Oh, I miss you all right! I miss so many people in my life! But, no one is forgotten...no memory fades away forever. No moment is abandoned in an attempt to make room for more. There is always room for MORE...if we allow ourselves the opportunity to grow as the willow, bending with the wind instead of struggling against the changing tides.

Change will always be a part of our life...and probably a part of your life, too. Change is new beginnings and old endings, all packed in together. Change is sorting and sifting and beginning again and again. It is clinging to what becomes familiar and letting go of that familiarity so we do not grow complacent and stagnant.

Change and moving and growing and helloing and good-bye are all a part of us. We each bring our history with us, wherever we are going. We can bring with us all the pain and hurt and terror of losing someone or we can bring the warmth and security and wonderfulness of loving someone. The choice is up to us. The path is ours to choose.

I'll miss the northern prairie. I really will! The landscape may be FLAT and the wind may be strong, but the people are my friends and our footprints shall remain...we did a lot of dancing in the dark up there! Maybe none of us knows the way...maybe that's the truth we're all search-ing for...you don't have to know where you are going as long as you know where you have been. Maybe it is the journey that is the prize...not the destination. Maybe roots grow deep INSIDE A PERSON rather than in A PLACE...maybe hurt and pain and love and laughter belong together so we can distinguish the good places from the lesser ones.

Maybe moving isn't such a bad alternative to house cleaning and maybe the boxes will find us and we'll start (again) to carve out a new beginning...bringing all of our yesterdays with us, but never letting them rob us of our NOW. I guess I carry it all WITH ME…inside my heart where there is no need for sorting and separating and packing and unpacking boxes of life. It's just ALL THERE ALWAYS…waiting for me to claim it as my own…waiting for a new footprint in a very old shoe.

Good-bye northern prairie…you've been WONDERFUL for me and I will carry you and your spirit with me always. But, maybe the word isn't GOOD-BYE…maybe it's UNTIL WE MEET AGAIN…if only in my thoughts and dreams and memories. Maybe I'm in yours too…

The moving van is lumbering somewhere behind me, bringing all our memories to wherever we will soon call home. But, in the meantime, I've got my ear flap hat on and one of the pink flamingos in the back seat so home won't be so empty when we arrive.

Hiding Places...
Safe Places

I need a place to HIDE. I need a place where NO ONE CAN FIND ME. Or hear me, or see me or touch me or reach me...or worry about me. I need a place, some place far away where I can go to when the rest of the world gets crazier than I am. I need a SAFE HAVEN...a resting stop along the way, an island.

I need a place where I can cry, yell, scream, eat a whole box of Oreos or wallow in melted chocolate if I want to. I need a place where no one cares if I wear white shoes before Easter, don't fit in a ONE SIZE FITS ALL bikini or keep my bunny slippers on ALL DAY. I need a hole where I can hide...a place I can crawl to when my feet won't carry me anymore.

There would be no alarm clocks, telephone, bills, calories or pain. The only sounds would be the ones I want to hear: waves crashing or lapping on the beach (depending upon my mood), the breeze rustling through trees that didn't need pruning, the gentleness of a ceiling fan that didn't need dusting. It would smell good, too. Maybe cinnamon or almond or wild flowers would greet my senses...maybe the dampness of a summer rain shower would float by or the fresh scent of newly mowed grass.

This hiding place would have no mailbox, front door or washing machine. There would be no TO DO LIST and the only thing in the RULE BOOK would be a smudge where someone erased all the other rules. It would be a perfect place...if only I could get there.

I want...no, today, I NEED a hiding place. When the emotions get mixed up and start to leak out the corners of my eyes and dribble down my cheeks, I NEED a hiding place. I don't want anyone to know I'm_____ (you fill in the blank) but sometimes, I just don't have the energy to hold up the mask any more and my secret is out. Where can you go when the memories rush back and the tears flood out, making pools on the desk in front of you? Where can you go when the anger reaches way past the SEEPING POINT and threatens to bust out of every pore? Where can you go when the guilt seems to glow from every fiber of your being?

Isn't there a PRIVATE PLACE where anger can be met and released without fear of reprisal? Isn't there a private club or corner or space where pain can be thrashed about until it loses its power or guilt can be wrestled with until we are completely empty? Where can we go when the world crashes down upon us...in the middle of a completely ordinary day. Where can we go when the words and the tears rush out...completely out of control? Where is this SAFE PLACE?

IN YOUR CAR.

Unless you carpool (and after you became "bereaved" you probably noticed a decrease in the number of passengers anyway), your CAR appears to be the handiest SAFE PLACE for those of us who still suffer moments of pain, anger, guilt or any of the other emotional aspects of grief. Your car is usually available unless you have succumbed to the grief response of losing your mind...and can't remember where you parked your car. We can usually get to it quickly and once inside, it is OUR SPACE.

Sometimes, just sitting in the car helps. Sometimes just sitting there with the smell of leftover pizza, old sneakers and the stale perfume is enough. By rolling up the windows and turning on the air conditioner and the radio, we can escape even the sounds of OUGHT. If you scrunch down low enough in the seat, maybe no on will even see you sitting there in your car and for a few moments, we can truly escape the call of responsibility and SHOULD. If no one sees you sitting there, you aren't and we might gain a few moments of solitude before someone remembers THE CAR and comes searching for you...

Sometimes, the hard feelings come over us as we are cruising down the highway. Sometimes, the BAD feelings sweep over us as we turn down THAT ROAD or pass by THAT PLACE. Maybe it's a song on the radio that starts the tears flowing or perhaps a billboard sends our heart backward through memory.

Maybe it's the car ahead of us that is to blame. Perhaps it's the same

color or model…maybe it's the driver who looks so familiar. Maybe it's his driving (her?!) that sends us into hysteria…remembering our first driving lesson or our first kiss or whatever beckons just beyond consciousness.

We often use our car as an escape, getting in and driving off, in hopes of finding some place where hurt can't find us…only to discover that even the CAR may not be a place free of memories. Just when we think we might have discovered a safe haven, the car becomes another reminder of all the things we don't have any more. And then, we cry…even in paradise.

And the tears begin to trickle down the cheek…blurring my vision and causing a slight wavering to my steering. How many times have we missed the exit because tears blocked the sign? We grip the wheel and grow white knuckled in the attempt to halt the speeding memories from over-taking us. There are lots of people out on the highways crying and for many of us, it has nothing to do with the price of gas.

Sometimes it's not tears that overwhelm me behind the wheel. Some-times, anger wells up inside me, especially if I am late or lost or tired. I grow impatient with the drivers ahead of me in a traffic jam and sometimes find myself honking the horn a little too frequently. HONK! HONK! HONK! The very sound of a automobile horn shatters the calmness and seems to reflect the discord within my own life. It sounds GOOD, like a siren that tells everyone to GET OUT OF MY WAY. I'M HURT AND I NEED SOME HELP...some understanding, some patience.

We pound the wheel in frustration that comes out as anger but really reflects our helplessness. We wave at others drivers with our fingers, sending messages of support and concern...telling them what we think of the WHOLE NASTY SCENE.

We may cry or shout or sing or curse inside our car...because it appears to be the only place where we are safe from having to be what others need us to be. I don't have to be FINE in the privacy of my windowed car...I can be whatever I want to be...and no one will notice. As long as I don't look out the windows, I won't have to notice the stares of my fellow travelers...I can hide here in the safety of my vehicle...until I turn the key.

Cars carry us everywhere except where the hurting part of us wants to go. A car can't take me THERE. But sometimes I find myself just driving...not sure where I'm going, but knowing exactly where I want to go. Many drivers appear to be in a daze...some of them are grieving and some probably should never have been allowed to drive in the first place. It's just hard to tell which is which...and who is who.

Are all erratic drivers grieving? Probably not, but many of us are trying to get to work, school or home in addition to trying to find that safe place where memories don't hurt and tears aren't bitter.

Please be patient with us the next time you pass one of us grievers on the highway. We might be going too slow to suit your pain or too fast for your grief, but we are all in search of something...or some place.

My car...probably as close to paradise and safe haven and island of calm that I will ever get. And that in itself is a thought worth grieving. I'll be OK as long as I can't find the key I seem to have misplaced. So, I'll just sit here awhile, pretending I'm on my way to someplace called peace.

Stock up on tissues and you might want to modify your car a bit for the journey through grief...maybe we need to put the windshield wipers on the inside.

A Source of Comfort

When things are difficult or painful in my life, I often go to my refrigerator for comfort. It is perhaps one of the best friends I have…always available, never too busy to listen and never, ever criticizes my choices in life. It stands ready to dispense whatever I need in the way of support; veggies when I am feeling virtuous, chocolate when I'm not. It is there, for me, 24 hours a day…a beacon of stability in a world gone mad.

Have you ever looked at your refrigerator? Your refrigerator says a lot about who you are, what kind of life you live and what's important to you. It is a reflection of the family who lives within in their midst. It occupies a place of honor or one of neglect, reflecting the moods and temperaments of the house's inhabitants. It is both a barometer and a monument…telling stories of the people who open its doors and who graze its shelves in hopes of finding something they need or want.

It speaks a special language…the language of time. Even its shape and size and color messages about its history and its place within the family. It is a familiar as food itself and taken for granted. Everyone has a refrigerator…if you have a roof over your head, then it's a pretty safe bet that there's a refrigerator in your life.

And what does that appliance, that guardian of hope and disaster, say about you?

The door, opening either left or right, tells us if you are right or left handed or if you bought this model to fit its space. If it's a changeable door, that may whisper of other kitchens, other houses, other places in the universe that have been called home.

The color makes a fashion statement that also reflects the appliance's age. Almond is the basic color of the last 15 years; harvest yellow and avocado really speak of age; black glass is ultra-trendy and white is just plain OLD.

Of course, the type of refrigerator also speaks of its owners. Does your refrigerator have the freezer compartment on the top or the bottom? Or is your household a side-by-side type? Do you have an ice maker, a door that dispenses ice (crushed, or cubed), a selection of cold beverages or allows you to survey different areas of the interior, grazing for suitable snack items? Are the top corners rounded? Are you taller than your refrigerator? Do you have glass shelves, interchangeable compartments, an egg tray, veggie bins with adjustable temperature controls and door shelves that can hold those giant bottles of soda or 12 gallons of milk?

Refrigerators do hint at the number of people who open them...the smudge of fingerprints at varying heights tells a true tale (unless you have one of those anti-fingerprint surfaces...in which case, you do not have to require everyone to wear gloves when opening the door!) The contents also reveal numbers, tastes, economic status and the social life of the owners. A refrigerator stocked full of soda, apples, jelly, eggs, bacon and popsicles says FAMILY while one with a single bottle of water, a half-used jar of olives and a box of Twinkies says SINGLE more accurately than any social register.

Even the terminology you use when referring to this appliance, gives a hint about its owner. ICE BOXES haven't been around for a hundred years (or so it seems to the younger crowd!) but is still an oft-used term for some generations.

Your refrigerator reflects something else too...something besides your age, socio-economic status and your love life. A refrigerator is actually a story book, a family scrapbook, detailing the comings and goings of whoever shares its living space. A refrigerator is a bulletin board...the message center...the nerve center for the family. Notes, report cards, menus, schedules, bills to be paid, stories to be told are all somehow secured to the front and maybe the sides of this magic box...the one place where one is fairly certain EVERYONE will visit at least once a day!

The latest finger-painting is displayed along side the reminder from the dentist. Last month's electric bill is buried beneath this month's gas bill and bank statements. A note from the teacher flutters each time the door is opened, but hasn't caught the attention of the proper authority yet. Photographs grace the door, sometimes held in place with magnets, others taped to the smooth surface. Photographs cataloguing and chronicling the day to day doings of the people who live here.

It is almost as if we have peeked inside someone's dairy...each time we pause to "read" someone's refrigerator door. Here, neatly and sometimes not so neatly, are displayed the victories, triumphs and despairs of the human race.

Some refrigerators are clothed in hundreds of magnets, of every description. No small amount of surface must be allowed to be visible! Every kind of magnet imaginable has found its rightful home on that cold, steel door. Each one, perhaps, carefully selected for a particular person in that household. Do you have fruit or vegetable magnets? Flowers, animals, happy faces or miniature plaques with cute sayings? Do you have slogans, advertisements or reminder buttons holding your world together?

It all reflects YOU...the one who so carefully puts on the bright and cheerful face each morning...even though your own heart may be breaking or dying from frostbite. We may have our "public face" in order, but the door of our refrigerator is a far more accurate measure of our life.

Refrigerators have served as family albums, bulletin boards and sounding boards ever since they were invented. But how did the CAVEMAN ever organize his life or communicate with his family if he didn't have a refrigerator on which to tape his schedule? How did one remember which casserole to serve, which day to carpool and which body went where on which day? How did the world get along before the refrigerator was born?

If only refrigerators could talk! What tales they would tell: of late night snack raids, early morning worry sessions, of pain, triumph and despair. They would tell of the FIRST PLACE VICTORY in the 100 yard dash and of the wonderful evening at the PROM. Refrigerators could tell of the dry cleaning to be picked up after the wedding and of how many people brought tuna casseroles...

They reflect birth, kindergarten, 5th grade, the teen years, the searching times of bachelorhood, the poor years of the newly married. Their

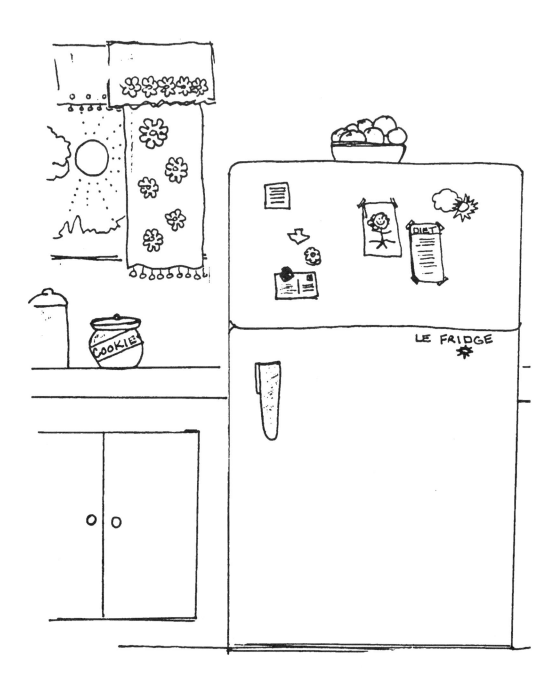

surfaces reflect the handprints of the young, reaching for grapes and the trembling of the hurting, reaching for comfort. Their surfaces have captured the passing of time, family and life. Their shelves have borne the weight of formula bottles, soda bottles, beer bottles and bottles of antacid. Pies, casseroles, fruit, an occasional vegetable and countless lunch boxes have rested within the cool shadows of the silent, yet vigilant refrigerator.

Do refrigerators have ears? Oh yes...they hear our laughter, our tears, our shouts, our whoops. They feel our poundings, our strength and our gentleness as we try to close the door so no one can awaken and discover the identity of the secret snacker.

And side by side, the birth announcement and the obituary hold our attention as we pass by. It neither weeps nor celebrates, this appliance that is so much a part of our lives...yet, it absorbs all of that and more...we lean against it in despair, pound it in frustration and slam it in anger. We ignore it and trust it...to keep us sustained in whatever hour we have a need.

We go to the refrigerator whenever we have thoughts to think. Somehow, things go better with milk, cookies, carrot sticks (you've got to be kidding!) Time seems to slip away into the night when we gaze at the shelves, searching for something to ease the feeling. The refrigerator becomes our companion in the darkness, feeding not just our bodies, but our sense of reality as well. It is a family history...an album...a reflection of where we have been and a display of hope for where we intend to go. Side by side, the birth announcement and the obituary...the refrigerator is part of it all.

The Mood

Sometimes, I'm in a BAD MOOD. Sometimes, I'm even in a TERRIBLE MOOD. And right now, I'm in one of THOSE moods. It's fall outside my window and it's winter inside my soul. I haven't felt much of anything for days and then, suddenly, it's as if the emptiness has been replaced by pure, clear, intense UGLY.

It's been a BAD day from the moment I thought about waking up and especially when the alarm clock decided for me. I got up on the wrong side of the bed, discovered we were out of toilet paper TOO LATE to do anything about it and then the toaster went crazy and I had to eat cold cereal without milk because that was bad, too.

The car keys hid themselves from my view, the dog wouldn't go out and once he did, he wouldn't come in. The sandwich makings were poor (NO ONE wants to eat anchovy paste and cream cheese!) and we were out of Twinkies. My panty hose ran, I had to catch the dog, my house mate "forgot" to take out the garbage (or was it my turn?) and when I did, the TOUGH SACK wasn't as tough as it needed to be…

It HAS NOT BEEN A GOOD DAY and it's only 8 a.m.

So, I'm in a BAD MOOD and I think I'll stay that way, today. Maybe I'll stay that way forever. All the lights were RED and everyone in front of me had nowhere else to go…S L O W must be the password for the day. I ran out of gas 3 blocks from work and I didn't FEEL like walking so I just sat there…no one stopped to help or to rescue me so I had to walk anyway.

There were 2,000 messages already on my desk when I finally got there and none of them were invitations for lunch. The calendar said I was already late for two meetings, neither of which I cared about or could even remember why I was supposed to be there. They were out of doughnuts at coffee break time and I discovered the ladies' room was out of paper TOO

LATE again!

I AM in a BAD MOOD and I don't want any one to cheer me up today. Someone did attempt a smile and I wanted to squash her face. Someone else told a joke and I guess everyone else thought it was great. I just wanted to be left alone. I shut my door, but the wind kept opening it and letting people in...people with smiles, people with stories, people with problems, people with paperwork...people, people, people...people sensing I  was in a BAD MOOD and tried to cheer me up. People with concerned looks on their faces and fleeting touches on my shoulder. But no one arrived with chocolate and no one nodded in agreement with my bad mood.

I wanted to be in my bad mood, but no one seemed to understand that. The more they tried to cheer me up, the worse it got. I wanted to scream and run away and stuff myself with forbidden treats and wallow in my anger, frustration, hostilities, my WHATEVER...so I left work early and pushed the car home (I really didn't, but I felt like it!). There were bills in the mailbox, nothing good in the refrigerator and an overdue notice from the library (I don't even remember going to the library, let alone reading something!)

I looked at the leaves piling up in the yard and thought about raking them and then didn't. I sat on the steps and just sank even further into my BAD MOOD. Oh, I know what to do when a BAD MOOD strikes. I know I should get moving, that exercise helps relieve the physical and sometimes even the mental tension of a bad mood. I know I should eat something nutritious and keep my blood sugar up without stuffing down a dozen doughnuts and I know the value of broccoli and a glass of milk. I know that music often soothes the painful spots and comforts the aches and I know that talking with an understanding friend often helps. And all of those things DO WORK…but right now, I don't WANT TO do any of those things!

I don't WANT TO…I want only the magic wand and the good fairy godmother and the glass slipper and fat-free chocolate. If I can't have paradise, then don't try to comfort me with anything else! Don't tell me to be grateful that I once loved or that time will heal the hurt or that something good is just around the corner (who can live that long!)

Sometimes, a BAD MOOD is just what I need and right now, A BAD MOOD is mine. You can't always be happy or cheerful or look on the bright side or believe in Tinkerbell or Santa Claus. Sometimes the tune goes sour and so does the milk. If only we knew that and believed that…and didn't try so hard to live each day as if it were our last (on days like this, that thought isn't so bad!). So what if this is my last day…sometimes that would be OK with me. I'm YELLING inside…why can't you hear me and let me be?

Those who would comfort us often try to cheer us up and out of our pain and sadness. How much more comforting if we were allowed to have awful days and not have to feel guilty about having them. I can't always be the cheerleader…even in my own life and I don't want to be either. I want to have a temper tantrum like the three year old down the block. She seems pretty OK to me most of the time…I am too.

But, once in awhile, nothing works and I don't have the energy or the will to pull the rabbit out of a hat anymore. And if I did, the rabbit would probably be dead anyway.

So, when a BAD MOOD strikes (and one will, believe me!) let it come and don't apologize for it. Don't cover it up, pretend it isn't there or hide from it. Like most other things in our lives, a bad mood is just that…a simple but awful feeling of despair and emptiness. We compound it by adding guilt, frustration and anger until what was simply a bad mood becomes a crisis, a permanent way of being, an emptiness that permeates the soul.

Just have the bad day…but do it WELL. Yell, cry, eat, don't eat, walk, run, or just sit. Whatever you do…DO IT. This may very well be your last day and why waste it worrying about how awful it is! JUST DO IT and don't worry about it.

Let the leaves accumulate…they will be there tomorrow too. Let the bills go one more day, but pay them tomorrow. Tomorrow is the thread that pulls us through these dark moods better than any other comfort. Tomorrow is the hope we cling to when the light bulb burns out and we run out of chocolate. THIS TOO SHALL PASS is my lifeline, but right now, let me be…please let me have my bad mood. It's mine and I have earned it.

Don't be afraid of it…respect it, learn from it, live it. Every cloud doesn't have a silver lining, glass slippers sometimes break and the cookie without calories tastes awful. If too many awful days seems to be strung together, then you'll have to do something about them, but if a BAD MOOD only strikes once in awhile, live it. Worry a little less and live a little more.

Without a tough day once in awhile, how would we recognize the good ones?

After All These Years, For That, I am Thankful

It doesn't seem to get any better, but it doesn't get any worse either.
> For that, I am thankful.

There are no more pictures to be taken, but there are memories
to be cherished.
> For that, I am thankful.

There is a missing chair at the table, but the circle of family gathers close.
> For that, I am thankful.

The turkey is smaller, but there is still stuffing.
> For that, I am thankful.

The days are shorter, but the nights are softer.
> For that, I am thankful.

The pain is still there, but it lasts only moments.
> For that, I am thankful.

The calendar still turns, the holidays still appear and they still cost too
much. And I am still here.
> For that, I am thankful.

The room is still empty, the soul still aches, but the heart remembers.
> For that, I am thankful.

The guests still come, the dishes pile up, but the dishwasher works.
> For that, I am thankful.

The name is still missing, the words still unspoken, but the
silence is shared.

> For that, I am thankful.

The snow still falls, the sled still waits, and the spirit still wants to.

> For that, I am thankful.

The stillness remains, but the sadness is smaller.

> For that I am thankful.

The moment is gone, but the love is forever.

> For THAT, I am blessed.
>
> For THAT, I am grateful…

Love was once (and still is) a part of my being…

> For THAT, I am living.

I am living…

> For THAT, I am thankful.

May your holidays be filled with reasons to be thankful…having loved
and having been loved is perhaps the most wondrous reason of all.

The Just Right Gift

Have you ever tried to wrap a present? I don't mean one of those nice, neat square boxes with something inside it. I mean, a PRESENT…one of those oddly shaped, too expensive, but JUST RIGHT things that leaps off the shelf and into your arms in the middle of August!

How come those things…the JUST RIGHT things are NEVER easy to wrap? They have odd little corners or big, poky edges that peek through the paper or start little tears that eventually become BIG RIPS and you have to start all over again. They have slippery sides and the paper wiggles around and the ends don't meet, no matter how large I cut the paper. The tape won't stick to those weird-shaped places that I think tape needs to go and no one can disguise the shapes on those JUST RIGHT presents.

Presents are very special in our family. They are the source of much discussion, stress and anguish. They are also a wonderful source of joy. Years ago, our family was normal in our pursuit of the JUST RIGHT gift for each member of the household. We would spend the prerequisite number of days dashing from store to store, in search of the JUST RIGHT GIFT, the one with the recipient's name "written on it."

Some of us were more creative than others and some of the gifts reflected not only the love with which it was given, but a sense of style, creativity or humor. Those gifts were easily wrapped and were often so beautifully gift wrapped that no one wanted to tear into them. So, gift giving became a long and tedious affair at our house…no paper could be TORN as one unwrapped one's gift. We would "ooh" and "ahhh" as each present made its debut and then the paper would be carefully smoothed, folded and put away for the next gift giving occasion. (Some would call this CHEAP, but we preferred to think of it as recycling).

Gift wrap wasn't the only thing that had to be handled gently, however. RIBBON was also a source of ritual in our house. Bows were simply plucked off the packages once everyone had admired them and stored in a zip-locked bag. Most of the bows still had the original sticky back label on them...we simply double folded tape on the back. These bows were still in their original condition!

Boxes, too, had their custom. Long before recycling became popular, our family simply used and reused the same boxes, year after year. After a while, you couldn't believe anything you read on ANY box! I once got really excited about receiving a blender only to discover my mother had packed a year's supply of new underwear inside. Shoe boxes were particularly popular although no one in our family had received shoes as a gift for years! Shoe boxes can hold all sorts of oddly shaped presents and they are pretty easy to wrap...even for the butterfingers in the family.

But then, one holiday season, no one thought much about gifts. We could barely breathe, let alone go shopping. The thought of being happy was beyond us. Our family had become lost in the despair of new grief and the only thing that sparkled THAT year were the tears in our eyes. Gifts? Who could think of gifts when the only thing we wanted was a return to yesterday. If you couldn't give us that, then don't bother!

From pumpkin time on, we could not bear the thought of surviving the holidays. How could we possibly endure the empty chair, the empty space, the emptiness? What gifts could possibly ease that kind of pain?

We tried. We tried to go shopping. But all we saw were things we didn't need to buy anymore. Everywhere we looked, we saw only what we didn't have...the emptiness and sadness echoed in every store, in every window, in every face.

Everyone else looked happy! And that seemed to hurt us even more. WHY couldn't we find that aisle marked HAPPINESS? Where were the GOOD TIMES? How could we wrap those and keep them alive forever?

That first holiday season wasn't so great. We did manage to stuff a turkey (I don't remember with what, however!) and I think we did decorate something. We dreaded the annual family gift exchange, though. How would we keep from sobbing and ruining the gift wrap? WHO CARED

about gifts and turkeys and traditions when OURS were gone!

It was that first holiday in the VALLEY, however, when we discovered the importance and endurance of love. Lost forever, or so it seemed, love came back as we struggled to survive. Unable to think clearly or rationally, unable to survive more than a few minutes at the malls, we did our gift giving differently.

As we sat together at the family gathering, we began to remember. Memories came painfully at first, but slowly, as the tears trickled down our faces, they turned from painful ones to the funny ones…to the look we loved so well, to the stupid remarks once said, the silly things once done. Cascading out of our hearts, came words and memories, all shared within the family circle. We laughed. We cried. We remembered and we shared.

The next season still found us almost unable to shop carefully. We would still forget where we parked the car and nothing on the shelves seemed quite right. HOW LONG DOES GRIEF LAST? Were we doomed to suffer forever, the pains and sadness of death? WOULD WE EVER BE HAPPY AGAIN?

That holiday the gifts and the givers began to change. No longer able to face the world and its concerns, we turned inward and fought to find some internal peace. In that search, the JUST RIGHT gifts began to emerge. We found a table centerpiece that would be JUST RIGHT for my sister and her husband. They entertained a great deal and this would be PERFECT! It was a plastic pineapple lamp, battery operated and surrounded by tiny fruits with little twinkle lights inside. When turned on, it glowed with a wondrous light…casting shadows of its leaves on the wall! It was SO BAD that it was JUST RIGHT! It seemed to "speak" to us and we couldn't resist its call…it seemed to sum up everything we felt…plastic, ridiculous, hopeless and out of place. We bought it.

Wrapping it gave us one of our real laughs. We couldn't find a box for it. We couldn't find any appropriate paper and what color ribbon does one put on a plastic pineapple lamp? We ended up putting it in a brown paper sack and tied it with a string. So much for TRADITION.

It was the hit of the holiday season and it still graces their table now and then. No one understands the significance of that awful plastic lamp, but our family remembers it as the first source of light in our newly re-claimed life. We know the heavens are enjoying it as much as we do! It was the JUST RIGHT gift that year.

And now…we have a NEW TRADITION. It has become a wonderful game for all of us. We search all year round for the JUST RIGHT gift for each other…the one that says "I THOUGHT ENOUGH TO SEND THE VERY WEIRDEST, AWFULEST, STRANGEST, TACKIEST GIFT I COULD FIND"…because we love each other and know that no earthly gift can ever match the gift of caring and love that we share with each other.

Gifts have ranged from a 25 pound green cement alligator to a stuffed pig that oinks Jingle Bells. We have searched until we have found a shell lamp that sings, a pitcher shaped like a radish and a flock of pink flamingos. Each gift reflects our family philosophy of pure, honest joy. While we used to search for a gift that impressed, now we know that a gift of love and laughter out last the sadness.

You can choose joy again…We can remember all the awfulness, the pain, the hurt, the emptiness of a loved one's death OR we can choose to celebrate the joy and the light they brought to our lives. We can count what we no longer have or cherish the wonder of the love we once knew. We choose joy and in that choice, we celebrate the love that never goes away.

So, if you cannot face gift giving this holiday season, try the simple gift of memory. And once you are comfortable with memories, try looking for the joy in them. JOY is everywhere and so is sadness. They do not cancel each other, but rather enhance the light. There is no light without shadow, but no shadow can happen without the light. Wrap that up…and save the paper, the ribbon and the box for next year.

Light in the January Gloom

It's January everywhere and for most of us, it is not the season of light. The season of light is past…lost in the mid-winter gloom of ice and snow. We managed to survive Thanksgiving, Hanukkah and Christmas and now, we are left with the emptiness and dread of the gray snow months…snow no longer light and fluffy, but grown icy and black with the soot and the earth's brown tinge. January is hardly the season of light for most of the world.

It is a time of reflection, of evaluating, of measuring ourselves against the yardsticks of progress. It is a time of planning, of making resolutions that will only be broken before they are even remembered and a time of wondering. It is a time of short days and longer nights…of icy winds and cold hands. It is a time when the light seems dim and distant and maybe just plain impossible.

WHEN IS IT GOING TO GET BETTER is the question we ask in January. When will IT stop hurting SO MUCH! Surely there must be a better prize for surviving the holiday madness than this empty feeling that creeps into our very bones in January! There must be light somewhere…but where and when will it return to my life!

January is often the month of despair and yet it marks the beginning of a new year…a fresh start, a chance to do it better or right or less often or more often or not at all. Surely it will get better THIS YEAR! Surely I won't hurt THIS MUCH this year! We search for some sign of hope in this month of icicles…some sign of magic that will keep us going until the warmth of spring arrives.

In what seems to be the longest month of the year, there seems to be little light. But that is what I want to think about now.

The SEASON of LIGHT.

The Seasons of Light began sometime shortly after you discovered breathing. From the moment you drew your first breath, light was a part of your life. Do you remember watching the stars at night while laying on your back in the backyard or at camp? Do you remember seeing the light in your parent's eyes as you performed at your first piano recital or participated in the spelling bee?

Can you remember your first love...and your second and your third? Do you remember the moment you discovered your partner was going to be more than just a casual companion? Do you remember the GLOW OF ANTICIPATION when you discovered you were going to have a baby?

Light has always been a part of your life. Remember birthday candles? Do you remember the look on your child's face when the candles were lit...or can you remember what you imagined that look would be?

The Seasons of Light...those moments when time stood still for a fraction of a second and are etched onto your soul: your first date, THE PROM, your wedding, your child's first step, his first words, her first smile. The first communion, date, learning to drive, graduation, wedding...your first grandchild...

The Seasons of Light...when life was in order...when the magic worked and for a moment...a single moment, happiness simply filled your life with light. You remember them...even now, even as they bring tears of remembrance. Or perhaps all you have are tears of anticipation because there were so few moments of light. But ALL OF US HAVE some memories...even if they are only brief ones in our imagination! There are memories of those quiet, private moments when you DREAMED of the light.

But now...those lights have gone out. Our loved ones have DIED and the lights are gone...never to twinkle again on this plane. The world has grown dark and cold and every month seems to be January.

WHAT'S THE USE of going on when there are no more lights to be lit? How are you going to make it through the darkness if there are no lights left for you?

I wish I had the answers! I cannot even guess at the depth of the darkness that must be within you at times. But, I do know that darkness does not have to last forever — even though it seems as though it does.

Yes, the light went out and the Seasons of Light seem to have grown dim. But it must be light somewhere! No matter how shattered your life, how fragmented your dreams, there must be light somewhere. There must be hope somewhere!

Our loved ones have DIED. We did not lose them or the love we share. Practice thinking and then saying...my child, wife, husband, mother, father, brother, sister, friend, DIED. Not "I lost my _____." OUR LOVED ONES ARE STILL AND ALWAYS WILL BE A PART OF US. WE CANNOT LOSE THEIR LOVE.

But sometimes, we think we do. Sometimes, we cannot remember the light. Sometimes, especially in the early months and even years of grief, all we can remember is the pain and horribleness of the death. Pain seems to overshadow everything. We will not erase that pain today…or ever. The pain of this darkness will always be with us, but it will change its intensity and its depth.

At first, all I could remember were the awful things. I kept track of all the things I didn't have any more and mental lists of the things I would never know or experience. But, as I LIVED THROUGH those memories, I discovered, that slowly, gently, those memories faded and were replaced, in time, with memories of his smile, his giggle, his LIFE DAYS, not HIS DEATH DAYS.

I began to remember that our son (and my mom) LIVED…not just that they DIED! Their LIGHT HAD GIVEN BIRTH TO OUR HAPPINESS AND ONCE I ACKNOWLEDGED THE DARKNESS, THE LIGHT COULD BEGIN TO PEEK THROUGH! Now, when I remember Austin and Mom, It is with JOY and WONDER and GRATEFULNESS THAT THEY WERE A PART OF OUR LIFE AT ALL!

So, this season of COLD LIGHT…

- Be PATIENT WITH YOURSELF. Do what you can and let it be enough. We live in a world of OUGHTS AND SHOULDS and suffer from GUILT because we cannot meet our own expectations. Be patient.

- Be REALISTIC. It will hurt, but don't try to block bad moments. Be ready for them. Let those hurting moments come, deal with them and let them go.

- Be KIND AND GENTLE AND FORGIVING of yourself. Figure out what you SHOULD do, balance it against what you CAN DO and the compromise. FORGIVE YOURSELF FOR LIVING.

- ASK FOR HELP WHEN YOU NEED IT.

- TAKE CARE OF YOURSELF PHYSICALLY. Eat right. Exercise. Jog your memory.

- WORK AT LIFTING DEPRESSION. Take responsibility for self. We cannot wait for someone else to turn on the lights. We have to do that for ourselves. Think of things you enjoy and give yourself a treat.

- LEARN TO LOOK FOR JOY IN THE MOMENT. Learn to celebrate what you do have…change the way you look at things. Get a pair of ROSE COLORED GLASSES.

- FIND THE LIGHT THAT YOUR LOVED ONE BROUGHT TO YOUR LIFE.

Find the music of your loved one and listen to it...again and again, if only in your memory. Our loved ones laughed and giggled and sang. Find that memory and tuck it away for the gloomy days.

LIVE THROUGH THE HURT SO THAT JOY CAN RETURN TO WARM YOUR HEART AND LIGHT YOUR LIFE.

So, build a bonfire and light it during this gloomy January and RE-MEMBER THE JOY THAT USED TO LIGHT YOUR HEART. Bask in the warmth of LOVE GIVEN AND RECEIVED.

LOOK FOR THE LIGHT...IT'S OUT THERE SOMEWHERE.

And may your January be kept warm with the light of your memories!

My Name Isn't Occupant

I got a bill today in the mail and that was ALL. Sometimes there are several envelopes inside my mailbox, but usually they turn out to be addressed to OCCUPANT. I guess that's me, but what I REALLY want is something addressed to ME, that is NOT a bill, an advertisement or a catalog.

I want a REAL piece of MAIL, a REAL letter…actual WORDS written on a piece of paper (or typed, I'm not picky!) that speak directly to ME. I want someone to tell me something about their life, share with me something fun or even ask me a question or two (besides HOW AM I DOING?) I want a reason to trudge (walk) down (or shovel down or slide down or swim down — depends on your geographic location) to the mailbox. I want a reason for ME to open the box. I want someone to remember ME!

Sometimes the silence in the world of the bereaved is just TOO LOUD. And I can't stand it anymore! I want to shout or yell or scream…just to see if there is ANY BODY left in the world besides me! I see other people on the streets and in the stores. I see faces and hear voices everywhere, but sometimes, it seems like NO ONE is looking for ME or talking to ME anymore. (I am sure they are talking ABOUT me, however!)

It's as though death made me invisible. At first, I thought death took away the one we loved. After a few weeks however, no one came by anymore (and after 6 months of loneliness, I would have even loved a TUNA CASSEROLE!) The cards and letters stopped. The food parade ended and the calls grew shorter and less frequent. And when someone did manage to reach me, we rarely (never is more accurate) spoke of my loved one. I learned early on in my grief journey, that death often does erase our loved one from the conversations and daily concerns of the rest of the world.

I didn't particularly like that, but I did adjust. I knew if I wanted a shared memory, I'd have to be the one to start the conversation. And after while, I did. I left the scrapbook out on the coffee table and I'd carry a picture with me — ready to bring up THE NAME whenever I could. I learned the "rules" of being bereaved and thought I had adapted pretty well.

I even managed the holidays and have survived the parade of hard dates: birthday, anniversary, death date, etc. I've grown accustomed to the

pace of grief (some days too fast, some days too black, others disappearing before I could catch them).

I've watched days slip through my fingers and others seem to last forever. Grief does become a familiar, if uncomfortable, companion.

But, what surprises me, what hurts me, is the SILENCE, the INVIS-IBILITY of ME. It's almost Valentine's Day and I worry that there won't be a single Valentine in my box...because no one remembers that even though my loved one died, I'M STILL HERE.

I want to write that in NEON. I AM STILL HERE! Didn't anyone ever notice ME or have I always been a part of someone else? Maybe I grew too close, blended too well. Maybe I was absorbed by my loved one. Are there any pictures of just me in the scrapbook?

It's the loneliness of grief that hurts so much for so long. It's the SILENCE that is SO LOUD. I don't mind the quietness of my life, but I DO mind the loss of friends who used to call, the mail that used to come, the light that used to glow. I ache for the sound of a voice calling MY name. I long for a letter addressed to ME, for something besides a bill in the mailbox. I hate the title OCCUPANT!

We know ourselves from the OUTSIDE IN and identify ourselves by others' perceptions. We introduce ourselves using our name, our title (Mr., Ms. ...I've always wanted to say QUEEN!). We hide behind our relationships (I'm a mom, a wife, a sister). When those identities are stripped away then we often have a difficult time identifying ourselves. Even the words we use to describe ourselves often come from others. Are you a GOOD wife (husband, mother,...)? Are you a STRONG dad, a LOVING sister, a PESKY brother?

Death seems to challenge all of those labels we normally use to identify ourselves, not only to others but to ourselves as well. Am I still a mother if there is no child to tuck in at night? Am I still a husband if there is no one to come home to? Am I still a sister, a brother, a friend...if there is no one to play with or tease anymore? WHO AM I NOW that someone I love has died?

It's a long and painful search for our new identity as we struggle through the Valley of Grief, but sometimes, that search seems terribly

LONELY as well as difficult. NO ONE calls anymore with invitations for lunch or a movie. NO ONE remembers any of my special dates or whether I like Oreos or Moon Pies. NO ONE sends me a card that just says "THINKING OF YOU" anymore. Did I die too?

It's the silence, the lack of first THAT ONE SPECIAL VOICE and later, lots of the voices that used to fill my world, that echoes so loudly now. I'M STILL HERE! I just am not sure who I am, or where I'm going or why I'm still around. But I AM...

And I want someone to know MY NAME ISN'T OCCUPANT.

I want a Valentine addressed to ME, not occupant. I AM...not an occupant in this life, but a real, hurting, grieving, LIVING person. I AM ME and I'M STILL HERE!

I have many labels, titles and identities. Some of them I like and enjoy, others I wish were not yet a part of my life (I'm bereaved is one I could live without for a looooooooooong time!), but I AM HERE and MY NAME ISN'T OCCUPANT!

Somewhere It's Spring

It's spring in some places now. And in some places, it will be winter for another couple of weeks (months?) Somewhere the tulips are beginning to push through the soft earth and somewhere the birds are returning to sing. Somewhere the air is warmer, the breezes more gentle, the land begins to awaken from a frozen sleep. The trees are beginning to bud and even the air smells fresh and clean.

Somewhere windows are open and the sound of the vacuum can be heard, marking the beginning of spring cleaning...a ritual given to us long before our forefathers set sail for a new world. Somewhere the last holiday decoration is being packed away (those holiday diehards!) and somewhere a lawn mower is being readied for a new season. Baseballs and bats are reappearing as skates and skis make their way to the basement. Somewhere stew pots are being packed away to make room for the salad bowls as we even change our eating habits from winter stuffing to spring sandwiches. And somewhere, maybe even a early "barbequer" is dreaming of sizzling steaks, grilled hot dogs and the season's first smoky session.

As spring approaches, we begin to shed our overcoats and stand in front of the mirror...examining the body for the extra lumps we've accumulated during the hibernation season. We lace up our jogging shoes and make our way to the sidewalks, high school tracks and to the gym, eager to strip away the added inches that came because it was dark, and gloomy and food seemed to soothe and comfort during the dark days of winter.

Somewhere someone is planning a wedding, a graduation, a family reunion. Vacation brochures begin to appear and plans are discussed in anticipation of summer. Snow boots are replaced by rain boots, sneakers take the place of mucklucks (a northern term for BIG BOOTS) and sweaters will suffice instead of parkas.

Spring is the reawakening season...the great WAKE UP CALL for the earth. Somewhere, someone is answering that get up call...greeting the new season with vim, vigor and vitality. There are smiles and renewed energy and hope seems to simply float on the softened air. Somewhere...all that is occurring, but not within me.

It's still snowing inside my being. It's still winter inside here and there aren't any tulips about to burst open in my spirit. I've still got my snow boots on and the sun hasn't quite made it to my world. It's still winter inside me...I wonder if spring will ever come?

Oh, there have been moments of spring in the past. Wonderful, warm, fleeting MOMENTS. Moments when I "forgot" about the pain, the emptiness, the despair, the grief. Moments when the world was right side up and the music made me dance. But, they were only moments and I'm still waiting for the forever good feelings to come back. I'm still waiting for spring to arrive in me.

It's been a hard winter and I'm weary of the gloom. Yet, I cannot seem to shake it off. The snow just doesn't sweep away, no matter how long I scrape the icy windows or work at lifting the depression. It seems as though I'm caught in a web of despair and spring cleaning has not erased the cobwebs from my heart. I CAN'T GET OVER THIS! I think I want to, but I wonder where HOPE HAS GONE.

Hope...the major ingredient in spring, seems to elude my grasp. Just when I think there might be some hope, a memory comes creeping across my soul and it's winter again in my heart. I haven't had a memory free of pain in what seems like a looooong time. Where are the GOOD TIMES? WHEN WILL IT BE SPRING FOR ME AGAIN?

It's this lack of hope that seems especially cruel during spring time. I thought this winter inside me would end and I was looking forward to a more peaceful time in my life. I thought we would settle down, plant a garden and live our life filled with memories and the opportunity to make new ones. HA! I thought grief would end at SOME POINT. The books all say it will...everyone else LOOKS like their griefs have subsided...how come spring missed us?!

I don't even have the energy to go looking for happiness. If it can't

show up on my doorstep, ready for the asking, then I guess I'll never be happy again. It just takes too much energy to plant the flowers, water and weed them and then discover I planted the bulbs upside down! Just my luck! It's my lot in life, my punishment, my dark cloud that follows me...my-whatever-went-wrong-in-the-first-place-and-now-will-continue-the-rest-of-my-life-luck!

A season without hope is the ultimate in despair and I've spent too many such seasons. I want the warmth of the spring air to blow past my windows too. WHERE DOES HOPE GO AND HOW DO I GET IT BACK?

Hope is that elusive something that keeps us moving, even in the dark. When the pioneers ventured westward, with all their worldly possession in a small wagon, hope was their leader. And as they faced challenge after challenge, lack of water, fierce enemies, endless prairie and sickness, hope was their guiding star. survival became the task and hope for a better day, a better horizon, a better piece of land over the next hill, became the motivator.

When the pioneer farmer stood on his newly claimed, but rocky land, he must have felt the same despair that sometimes permeates me. All of his life had been left behind in search of something new and wonderful and for all of his troubles, he laid claim to a piece of rock strewn prairie. What luck! He must have felt helpless and powerless in the face of the enormous challenge. Grief surely must have ridden in those pioneering wagons!

But, as the farmer stooped to move the first rock from his land, perhaps hope began to return. For he had a vision of what this land could be. As he grabbed a stick and began to scrape the earth, hope began to grow once more. As he cleared the earth with his bare hands, the feeling of helplessness faded and was slowly, painfully, replaced by the hope for his dreams. Some day...somehow, this barren piece of earth would become a farm, bearing the fruits of the pioneer farmers' labors. He was, at first, helpless and lost in despair. But, with the simple act of bending over to move that first rock, he moved from helplessness to hope.

We are only powerless when we have no hope, no vision, no faith in our own abilities. We may be helpless at times. We may question the arrival of spring, but we are only truly powerless when we have no hope, no dreams to bend us over to pick up the first rock.

There are times in our life when spring seems far away and perhaps spring is the farthest away when we demand its return. We keep looking for the DAYS and WEEKS and MONTHS and YEARS of feeling good. We keep demanding perfect days, all strung together to make a good life. We keep kicking the rocks instead of bending over to pick them up and MOVE THEM.

We keep waiting for the SEASON of DESPAIR to end and end up missing the moments when despair is less. We keep demanding that it always be light, always be pleasant, always be pain free. And if we can't find those magical times when springs reigns supreme, then we cast away whatever it is we do have...rejecting the moments of lightness because we wanted DAYS of happiness, not mere moments.

Somewhere it IS spring and somewhere it isn't. But, it can be spring inside us if we will let it begin. Spring begins with a remembered joy, a cherished moment when we allow a spark of happiness to permeate the gloom. When we are mourning intensely, if that tiny spark of joy can be ignited for only a few seconds, we know there is hope. And hope is the opposite of helplessness which is reflected in our anger, in our guilt and in our sadness.

Don't lose the hope! Search for it! Fight for it! DEMAND its return. Hope changes as we do and it can be so disguised that we may not recognize it, but it can be found — in the MOMENTS of our memories. We probably won't ever have totally happy lives again...but so what?! We probably didn't have that kind of life anyway, we just thought we did. In our pain, we often paint in brighter colors than reality did. We keep demanding that our life return to its past happiness and we lose hope as we discover that isn't possible.

Bend over! Pick up a rock! Move it! Find new moments to cherish, blending them in with the old to mend the torn fabric of our lives with tiny stitches, each one made with joy and remembered laughter. Demand less of yourself and accept more. Search for the MOMENTS, don't wait for the years of happiness!

Don't let death rob your of the moments of joy still be remembered, to be found. Don't let grief rob you of those SPRING PLACES where love and joy live forever in the heart.

Somewhere it IS spring...Deal with the anger, the guilt, the depression as it comes and then let it go as you can...so there is room for joy to come again. Let hope come in...it's spring.

Songs of Life

I used to hum a lot. I hummed while I did the dishes, made the beds and folded laundry. I carried a tune with me as I climbed the stairs to the attic and foraged in the basement. Snatches of songs accompanied the drone of the vacuum cleaner and filtered through the shower noise.

My mother used to hum too. In fact, as I grew up, I noticed quite a few people in my world seemed to have an internal dance band directing their movements. My sister and I used to hum while setting the table and after dinner, we often broke into chorus while Dad played the piano. We had sing-along sessions that seemed to speed along the chores. Dad would play the "wild stuff" and then Mom would take over the keys, filling our house with the drama of Beethoven, the gentleness of Mozart and the pure joy of her own compositions. There was always music somewhere in our family.

As a teenager, I discovered the radio and followed my sister's travels into rock 'n' roll and other sounds that weren't always acknowledged by our parents as music. We read to music, danced to the radio, dressed to tunes, showered to the current "hits" and even studied to the rhythms of our generation. In fact, studying to the sounds of silence was simply unheard of.

A radio was second only to a mirror as the most important accessory in a car! We used to entertain ourselves on long car trips by singing every camp song we knew, but later, the car radio kept us awake.

Music was always a part of my life. From the humming we did during chores to singing around a campfire to the thousands (millions?!) of hours spent in piano lessons to the lullabies I sang to my own children, music accompanied the rhythms of my life.

My husband and I once cleared a dance floor with our rendition of "Zorba, the Greek" and my dad told me he could "definitely hear me" as I performed with the "Angel Chorus" in kindergarten! We started our marriage with music and although the tunes and sounds have changed, the music continues.

I'm not sure music has always accompanied MANKIND, but surely it has become a reflection of our emotions. We move to a thousand different rhythms, each listening to his own song, his own pattern. Sometimes we join songs, sometimes we are solitary in our dance. But always, there is sound.

Music knows no time frames and a song can transport us to wherever memory plays the tune. Hearing an old favorite can bring back not only the physical sense of "being there", but the emotional experience as well. Hearing "our song" can bring a smile or tears...as the pages of the mental scrapbook are turned once again. We are transported back across the years and often find ourselves temporarily reliving the scenes so anchored with that music.

We may find ourselves crying over a song on the radio, remembering the moments when that song spoke to our heart. We may find a smile flickering across our souls, as certain words and notes reach deep into memory to highlight a special moment. The wonderful birthday party, the moment when love was first acknowledged, the peace of some melodies, the pain of others...all come flooding back when the music plays. It is as if time had never passed and we are once again, young, foolish, in love, in sorrow, lost, found or whatever we were when THAT SONG played.

Music somehow reaches beyond the mind and finds those places that we keep secret, even from ourselves. It stretches beyond the carefully erected walls and sneaks past the buried pieces. It touches us as nothing else can.

But sometimes, the music grows still. I stopped humming once. The music simply died. There were no sounds, it seemed. Even my mother's gentle humming of a long cherished lullaby could not reach the stillness that death brought. Perhaps there was song, but I could not hear the music...grief had stolen away the notes.

I moved to no rhythm. We stumbled, fell and simply lay numb across the earth. The music had died.

But my mother refused to let the songs go. Gently, persistently, lovingly, she kept the sounds alive. Whenever she would visit, she hummed as she washed the dishes, hummed while she weeded my neglected garden and rocked us all in her arms. Knowingly, she refused to let the silence win and she wound the music box, so painfully silent.

She caught us by surprise with her piano playing one night and as our still aching daughter tried to move her grief stricken body to its tantalizing tones, we too, were drawn into the healing sounds. How long it had been since joyful sounds had echoed in our hearts!

NO one understood our pain, yet my mother brought the music back. She sang again the camp songs, the ones I had whispered to HIM as we rocked our way through such sick and endless nights. Death had stolen not only our light, but our sound as well and it was my mother who brought it back.

Our voices were shaky (some still are), but as we let the humming come back, we found the memories of happier times returning as well. We chuckled as we remembered our own car trips — singing at the top of our lungs, making up the words when we couldn't remember the right ones. We remembered the Happy Birthday Song and the lullabies and the "I'm scared so let's sing" songs.

In her wisdom, my mother knew the silence wouldn't last forever, but that we sometimes need some help in picking up the tune again. She simply refused to let death steal away the songs. We sang while we played. We sang while we worked. We sang while we cried and we healed as we sang.

Even as death began to still my mother's voice, she refused to grow silent. She hummed and when that was gone, she tapped her fingers to some secret melody. And finally, only her eyes danced, but dance they did! Just like HIS had!

Did they both hear a song of life that we could not imagine? Are there songs yet to be sung, with words I do not know?

Can you hear the music of your own self? Sometimes joyous, sometimes sad, sometimes so silent the emptiness echoes? Listen! Grow still in your frantic flight from pain and find the music of your memories. Death may have stolen the arms that used to hold us, but even death cannot still the sounds of love given and received.

Is it any wonder, when on a still and silent night, we can almost hear the heavens humming? It's LIFE still singing...endless voices, humming, singing, bellowing, crying, laughing, living.

It's Pachelbel's Canon, Beethoven's 5th, the first grade choir, heavy metal and Lawrence Welk all rolled into one magical song...of love.

"Not Quite Right"

It doesn't fit anymore! That's the cry heard 'round the world in June. It doesn't fit anymore. It's either TOO SMALL, TOO BIG, TOO TIGHT, TOO LOOSE, TOO LONG, TOO SHORT…TOO SOMETHING, but NOT QUITE RIGHT ANYMORE.

The bathing suit I bought last winter (on sale) just doesn't fit the way it did in the store (I won't tell you which TOO it is…). It doesn't feel "quite right" and it sure doesn't look like it did on the mannequin! It looked WONDERFUL on her. Even my facial expression can't come close to hers…there are no tears stains on her cheeks.

And HIS stuff doesn't fit "quite right" this summer either. The shorts we packed away last fall don't "feel right" and they don't cover as much as they used too. The material isn't as bright and the stripes seem to be turned the wrong direction…

The curtains are wrong, too. Instead of draping beautifully along the window's edge, they don't hang "quite right" and now they just look heavy, dreary and out of place. And the bedspread needs to be lighter. I'm tired of the winter plaid and I'm drifting towards pink flamingos and chenille. That certainly doesn't look "quite right" in winter (and probably won't look any better in June, but I am partial to flamingos.)

The living room needs rearranging and we could certainly dump THAT chair. We could use new slipcovers, but it might be easier just to get a new couch. After all, there are plenty of miles on those cushions and as long as we are celebrating the arrival of summer with a clean sweep…how about summer white canvas with navy blue stripes?

We could store the dining room table away for a few months and put a patio set in its place. It would change the look of the room although we might have some difficulty with the umbrella and the ceiling fixture. I want new carpeting, too. This all purpose beige no longer reminds me of beach sand (although it now feels a bit like sand). I want summer green or peach blossom beneath our new furniture. And white wicker and lots of plants — REAL plants instead of those silk ones. Let's change everything! It's summer.

It's summer and I want a new look. Nothing from last winter or even left over from spring seems "quite right" now. Clothes don't fit. Furniture doesn't "fit". Even the rhythms and routine of our life don't seem "quite right" in the summertime. I want a new look, a new feel, a new me.

I want ice cream with no calories (or fat...now you know why the clothes don't fit). I want dust free curtains at the sparkling windows and carefree slipcovers over stain-free chairs. I want fresh fruit and bananas that don't go black overnight. I want cool breezes blowing (but not at gale force) and lovely music drifting over the pond (what pond?!). I want a willow tree in the front yard and grass that looks better than the Easter basket stuff but doesn't require any work.

I want flowers that bloom continuously without tending and a garden that is weed-free and bountiful. I want to feel better, look better and to be better...in the summertime. I want to shed the overcoat, put away the boots and hang out the "Gone Fishin'" sign. I want to bicycle away the hours on a lazy afternoon instead of balancing the checkbook and I want all pens to run out of ink just as I begin to jot down my chore list!

June is the beginning of summer and the end of all other seasons. We need new clothes, flowers, furniture and thinking for the warm, gentle months of summer. What got us through the winter may not work "quite right" in the breeziness of summertime. The music changes and even the clock seems to slow down a bit. Time is measured in hops and skips rather than slippery steps and staggering plods. The day wakes up earlier and stays later in the evening and the fireflies dance through the twilight. We spend more time on the porch and less time in the basement in summer. We eat lighter and cook out more. We sing more, dance more and maybe even laugh more. Anger seems out of place and so does grief. It doesn't fit "quite right" in the season where we can't hide beneath the blankets and quilts. They've been stored away in the moth balls and it seems as though the world would like us to tuck away the hurt and pain of our grief seasons as well.

But with every creak of the wicker rocker, with every cast of the fly rod, the memories come racing back, catching me off guard and clouding the day. Pain doesn't fit "quite right" in the heat of a lazy summer afternoon, but sometimes, the memories drift home and it does hurt. It hurts to remember the late night story times that are no more. It hurts to recall the garden that now only grows weary weeds. It hurts to count the stars on a summer's night and find two more that I know by name.

Grief can withstand the hottest nights and thrive in the brightest of

suns, but it seems particularly cruel in the seasons of summer. One set of footprints in the sand…one fishing pole…one popsicle instead of two.

I want some peace in this season of play and I guess I can't wait for it to come to me. I'll have to go in search of the magic wand myself. If joy isn't in new slipcovers or a bathing suit that doesn't fit "quite right" because it's TOO BIG then I'll just have to create it for myself. The rocker is still on the porch, the fishing pole still waits. It's up to me to set the sails in new directions.

And so I will. I'll learn new dances, hike new trails, try new (low fat) foods. The garden needs weeding and I can wipe away tears as I wipe away the weeds that threaten to choke out the joy that garden used to bring. It's summer. It's JUNE. It's graduation day, wedding day, moving day, summer day. It's hello and good-bye, all said in the same breath and cast into memory as grief. Grief never feels "quite right", no matter what the season. So, I'll try to quit worrying and stop putting it away in moth balls.

Grief belongs in any season where love grows. But it isn't the only legacy of love…memory too belongs in all seasons. And it is up to us to nurture the joy and honor the pain, even if it doesn't fit "quite right". Cherish it all in this summertime of life. Thank heavens there are footprints to remember!

The Other Side of Grief

I used to search for rainbows. They were special symbols for us. Our son, BIG A, died during the night in a fierce thunderstorm and as the dawn broke, the storm ended. As we emerged from the house, we were greeted by a beautiful rainbow spanning the mountains outside of Denver. We felt it was a message from BIG A and from GOD that he had made the journey and was all right and that we would be too. So, rainbows have been special to us. And we searched for them to remind us of BIG A.

We began to collect rainbows. People sent us rainbow items and eventually, our house began to look like a rainbow gift shop! We had rainbow dish towels, bath towels, pictures, shower curtain, tea pot, hot pads, toilet seat cover, jewelry, artwork and best of all, rainbow toilet paper (for special occasions). I wore a small enameled rainbow on a gold chain around my neck and never went anywhere without it.

We spoke to rainbows whenever they appeared. Just a quick "Hey there, BIG A" or maybe just a wave or later on, a glance and a smile were enough. But we always acknowledged the presence of our rainbow child and said a silent prayer of thankfulness for the reminder of our love.

Incredibly, rainbows came to us on Big A's birthday and again on his death date for the first 5 year after his death. They were symbols and we clung to them.

For five years, rainbows somehow peeked through the incredible weight of those days and helped to ease the painful memories into gentle reminders of the love we shared, of the love we still have.

We grew comfortable in our yearly ritual and by year four, had begun to release a lot of the pain of our son's death. I still wore the rainbow as a constant reminder and we grew more confident in our ability to "handle"

our grief. It all hinged, however, on seeing a rainbow on those two important days during the year. We could go for days and maybe even a week or so without much pain as long as we knew our rainbow would be coming eventually. We grew dependent upon those outward symbols of our son's life to keep us close to the joy we had known. Without those tangible reminders, we tended to sink into despair and remembered FIRST the details of his life's struggles.

At year six, however, the sky was too clear and I sensed a change was coming. We lived in southern Texas and September dawned bright and hot and clear. I panicked. I didn't WANT to change. I'd already changed ENOUGH! His birthday was a warm September day, with no traces of clouds or rain. But I remained confident...after all, we'd gotten a rainbow on this day for five years. Why shouldn't I expect one this year, too? Besides, I NEEDED a little boost this year...it had been harder than I had expected.

And so, I went through the DAY, always glancing at the sky. My mind wandered through the memories of BIG A's life and other family members called to share thoughts throughout the day. By 10 p.m. I sat on the front stoop and WAITED. By 11:30 p.m. I was lost and at 12:01 a.m. the NEXT DAY, I cried. No rainbow had come.

We didn't get a rainbow on his death date either. As much as I wanted a rainbow to come, as much as I NEEDED a rainbow to appear out of the hot, cloudless September day, the sky remained clear at year six. Good-bye happened all over again.

GOOD-BYE??? I wasn't through saying HELLO!!!

We grieved all over again…this time for the skywash that had held out the promise of HOPE all these years. If only we would get our rainbow on those important dates, then we could cope the rest of the year with the loneliness, the despair, the pain that although different, was still there. I ached again, longing for my rainbow to come and remind me that our life with BIG A really did happen. It was as if he died all over again this year.

And so we retreated back into grief, a long time companion. But something else happened that year. Just as we retraced our steps through the valley, we noticed our despair felt different. It seemed to last a shorter length of time…the gloom seemed to fade more quickly whenever it came. We did laugh more often in spite of our renewed grief.

I wrestled long and hard and finally discovered the awful truth of grief…my loved one, our beloved son, had died, but we had not. We were left among the living, left to carve out an existence that had to endure not only the pains of life, but the joys as well. And suddenly, survival wasn't enough. If we were to be stuck in life, then we wanted to LIVE again.

I didn't want to remember only the awfulness of his death. I wanted to recall the joys, the light he brought, the music of his presence in our life. Slowly, painfully, we learned we did not need the symbols to remind us of our son and the joy and love we share. We learned to release the darkness in hopes of there being light in spite of the terribleness of the storms we endured!

Some say the path to healing (I do not like the word RECOVERY — sounds too medical to me. I can recover from a broken arm or the chicken pox, but recovery from grief just doesn't seem to "fit") begins when we learn to say good-bye. Good-bye to what? To whom? Good-bye to our loved one? I think not! I can say good-bye to the life we lived together, but never, ever to the memories and the moments of the life we shared! I can pick and choose how those memories affect me and just knowing I have choices is the beginning of the OTHER SIDE OF GRIEF.

Most of us still TIME FRAMES against which we measure ourselves. See if you can think about letting those OUGHTS and SHOULDS and time frames go. See if you can say good-bye to those dictates. See if you can LIVE YOUR GRIEF INSTEAD OF JUST SURVIVING IT.

Live your grief with all the passion you once lived your life. Even the shadows have something to explore and to learn about. Even the pain tells us something. Experience the hurts, acknowledge the pain, let the tears flow. If we can allow ourselves to experience and express the painful and deep emotions of grief, then we may gradually become aware that the well of hurt is not quite so full. The intensity and duration of the pain has changed as we have lived it. When once we hurt continuously perhaps now you are discovering a few moments of respite from the searing heat. Perhaps smiles come more easily when the memories flood in. Perhaps you have learned to cry and laugh at the same time.

Don't postpone, deny, cover up or run away from your pain. Be with the pain...NOW...everything else can wait. An emotional wound requires the same priority attention as a physical wound. Set time aside for mourning.

The OTHER SIDE OF GRIEF is not freedom from pain nor is it a return to the original picture or dream. It is acknowledging and living your grief. It is finally understanding that we DON'T GET OVER GRIEF. WE GET THROUGH IT.

The heart can mend the hurt and learn to grow and expand, not crumble and die, never to love again. It's to love life once again, despite the twinges of hurt and the catches of pain that will grab hold of us on occasion the rest of our lives.

Now as you look back, it is amazing to see the LIFE FABRIC, no longer ripped apart with a gaping hole, but mended with tiny stitches. Left perhaps a bit lumpy, patched with time, effort and love. The fabric of our lives has many tears and just as many mends. Old threads and new ones have blended together and have been re-woven into a pattern not quite the same as we had originally planned. It becomes a TAPESTRY OF LOVE...our history, to pull around us in time of need, to keep us warm, to shelter us from the storms and to comfort us in the trials.

I used to think Big A's life was just last week, but now I can count the years accurately. Now I know his life is intertwined with mine and "just last week" has become always...now...within.

I have come to know that in letting go of the hurt, I have gained all the wonderfulness that was Austin's life. Our son lived his life surrounded with love and joy. He filled our life with happiness and music. He lived his life at the top of his lungs. I can do no less in his memory.

He brought light to our life. He laughed and giggled and sang. So did your loved ones. FIND THAT MUSIC AGAIN.

Listen...the summer breeze carries the sounds of remembered love.

Capture it! Carry it always in your heart. The sounds of love cannot fade.

I don't need to wait for rainbows to come any more! The rainbow really lives WITHIN ME. That's the OTHER SIDE OF GRIEF...

I Slipped Backwards

Islipped backwards today. I ate a cookie. I did not run my 2.5 miles. I did not cross off every item on my TO DO LIST. In fact, I added things. I slipped backwards today. I put on a record, got out the scrapbook and slipped backwards into yesterday...into a hundred yesterdays where life was different than it is now. I slipped backwards as I "forgot" to do my exercises. And my whole IMPROVEMENT PROJECT was lost.

Today was just like any other day EXCEPT that I slipped. It started out OK, like most days do. Nothing special or extraordinary — just a day, another step in the endless succession of days. There were things to do, places to be, people to talk with, plans to dream about. It didn't feel especially different than any other DAY...but apparently it was and I slipped.

I've been doing "pretty good". In fact, I've become rather proud of myself in the last few months, beginning to take control of my actions, thoughts and life. I had finally figured out what it is I want to do and had developed a PLAN...I even wrote IT (the PLAN) down on a sheet of paper and taped it to the refrigerator so I could inspire myself every time I looked at it (and every time I went in search of something to nibble).

It was working, too. I've spent the summer living in POSITIVE POWER and things had begun to change. Productivity was up. Tissue use was down. Healthy choices were being made. Cookie raids were almost nonexistent. I WAS MAKING IT! Until today...when I slipped.

Maybe it was because the weather wasn't cooperating. It was supposed to be cooler and it wasn't. I'm weary of summer's heat and I was looking forward to the weatherman's promise of "slightly cooler". I seem to have more "courage" (will power?) when it's "slightly cooler" outside.

The calendar says ALMOST FALL and today, I guess I couldn't wait for ALMOST.

I am tired of being "kissed by the sun." I am tired of eating fruit and of sunny days. I'm tired of sand in my shoes and I'm tired of trying not to cry whenever I remember.

I slipped backwards today. I ran out of energy to keep up the GOOD WORK and I slipped.

I lost control and ate a cookie.

I slipped off the bandwagon of healthy and positive power and "I CAN." And I landed squarely in the middle of "I DON'T WANT TO" and "I CAN'T". I lost control and wept the tears of grief…mourned for the life I no longer live and grieved for the happiness I could only remember.

There are times when one grows weary of surviving, of being STRONG. There are times when cookies taste better than seaweed and

there are times when I WANT what I can no longer have...food wise, lifestyle wise, people wise. I KNOW I can't have those things, but I can still WANT them, can't I?

Usually, I am pretty responsible, but sometimes that means we are our own worse enemy...our own worst critic...our own judge, jury and jail term. I've live in the LAND OF OUGHTS for a whole summer now and the results are amazing...when I look in the mirror. But, sometimes, when I look in the heart, I wonder...if life is supposed to be so wonderful, then how come chocolate has calories, memories sometimes hurt and whatever I want to do, eat, think, or be isn't what I'm SUPPOSED to do, eat, think or be!

By now I SHOULD be happy and I usually am, although that has nothing to do with my memorizing THE BOOK OF SHOULD. It has to do with living, each moment, rather than wishing those moments would fade.

And today, I got tired and I slipped.

Today I slipped and ate a cookie.

I went backwards, but this time I knew it and I knew it was only for tonight...when the moon is full and the memories are warm. I knew it was only for the moment. I only ate one cookie...not an entire bag. I only cried for a few minutes...not an entire evening. I only let go of the shoulds for a little while...in order to discover the magic of memory.

I did the GRIEF SHUFFLE today and learned that even when we slip backwards, stumble, fall down or drift sideways for a time, we are making progress through the valley. ANY MOVEMENT is progress in the journey through THE VALLEY, even if that movement is in the opposite direction of where we thought we SHOULD BE GOING.

I slipped backwards. Today I celebrated my pain as a measure of my love instead of counting it as being a failure or an indication that I'm not OK yet. Today, I ate the cookie and tasted victory...I CHOSE to eat the cookie, to remember the moments, to cry, to hurt and to laugh.

Today I slipped backwards in THE IMPROVEMENT PROGRAM and moved ahead in living.

If I Could Just See Hope

I'm tired of waiting. I'm tired of waiting for the light to turn green, for my hair to grow out, for the cows to come home. I've BEEN waiting. How long does a red light last? I'm late and the traffic light knows it! I'm tired of waiting!

It wasn't really a BAD haircut. She said it would "grow out." But when? How many "bad hair days" must I endure? I'm tired of waiting.

And the cows...I guess they do come home eventually...if they have a home. I'm tired of waiting for the cows, too (although I hope they don't come home to my house!)

It's been a looooong journey. I thought it would end someday.

I really didn't have any particular day in mind or even a season or a year. I just thought it would end at some point in my life. I've been patient, waking each day with some glimmer of hope. I've been tolerant, learning to roll with the punches and to give when I really wanted to get.

I've learned the rules of the game. I know when the silence is required and when it is "safe" to allow my thoughts to be formed into spoken words. I've learned to dodge and dart, dancing as a boxer seeking to outlast his opponent.

The pain really isn't too bad any more. In fact, there are now days and even weeks when there is little more than a twinge to color my day. So unlike those first days, weeks and months! Now my footsteps almost have a spring to them sometimes. Before, they left deep imprints on the earth and even left a trace of a light drag of the left toe.

I used to be filled with ice water or lava...depending upon the thoughts that raced across my heart. I alternated between frozen or being consumed by flames. Grief is a difficult journey.

Guilt became a constant companion and I could hardly wait until the

day would come that I could cast the burden aside. I was patient, however, allowing each "if only" and each "I should have" to have its moment in my soul. Early on, I learned to listen to those "what ifs" and to respect them. They did have something to teach me, but I grew weary of the lessons. I wanted to cast them all aside. Others tried to help me dismiss those guilts with their kindly words. "You did everything you could" became a Band-Aid meant to keep me from drowning. But, in the end, I had to wrestle those demons myself and I had to reason with my own knowledge about doing everything possible.

Anger swept over me many times as I stumbled along the rocks and stones. Frustration built up inside me and I raged against the wind with clenched fist. "IT'S NOT FAIR!" became my battle cry. And the light stayed red.

Beneath the frustration grew an ever increasing sense of helplessness and that lead to a period of gloom. It was hard to keep going when the "I don't cares" took hold. There seemed no point in getting out of bed each morning or in returning to bed each evening. No one needed me. No one needed me to fix breakfast or to clean house or to earn money or even to come home. After all the plants died, even the plastic ones didn't need me. The cat left home in search of a fuller dish and the cobwebs grew well in the corners. No one needed me.

I must have changed my phone number because no one called and the mail dwindled down to a few bills and even fewer pieces addressed to "Occupant." The post office didn't need me. I became invisible except for the throbbing hurt in my heart. Even the cows got lost.

Despair, anger, guilt, loneliness, and pain all became familiar companions and then, too, left me. Left me to dance alone in the dark — only I couldn't remember the tune.

I grew tired of waiting for the music to start again. I waited a loooong time for my ship to come in. I kept hoping and watching, working and waiting. But the silence grew louder and then, even hope left.

I didn't know hope was so fragile. If I could just see the light at the end of the tunnel…if I could just see the last dirty dish, the last bill to be paid, the last weed to be pulled…IF I COULD JUST SEE HOPE, then I know I could go on…

And so I waited. I waited for the cows to come home and they did. And it was a mess. I waited for the light to change and it did. And everyone went at once and it was noisy. My ship came in, but hit the dock and sank at the end of the pier. I saw the light at the end of the tunnel. It was a train.

I kept waiting for someone to bring me happiness and it was never enough. I kept waiting for IT to get better and it only grew darker. The light was a TRAIN! I lost everything.

When there was nothing left, when I was all alone, I was still breathing. I tried to hold my breath, but it didn't work. The next breath always came and then the memories came, too. I found I could still remember a smile, a giggle, an US, a ME. Even when everything else was gone, there was still memory and there was still ME.

I began to remember that my loved one LIVED, not just that he died! His light had given birth to my happiness and ONCE I ACKNOWLEDGED THE DARKNESS, THE LIGHT COULD BEGIN TO PEEK THROUGH. As I lived THROUGH those memories, I discovered, that I could bring some of the happy memories back. Slowly, gently, over a long period of time, and with lots of work, the hard memories gave way to easier ones…his smile, his giggle, his LIFE DAYS, not his DEATH DAYS.

I finally figured out that I could make the music come back. I could remember the joy, I could remember the tune. I don't have to wait for someone else to bring me hope. Instead of looking for the light at the end of the tunnel, I know I can find the light within. I can rekindle the memories of love given and received. I can choose how those memories affect me. I don't have to drown or lose the light in the sadness of grief. The memories are mine and they are my light.

Happiness is not the absence of pain, but the possibility of joy returning…of memory becoming the light. I will cry forever, but I refuse to lose the joy we shared. I can laugh at the moment and remember the magic of US!

GRIEF ISN'T A SEASONAL SONG. IT'S A LIFETIME SONG, BUT IT DOESN'T HAVE TO BE A SAD SONG FOREVER.

LIVE THROUGH THE HURT SO THAT JOY CAN RETURN TO WARM YOUR HEART AND LIGHT YOUR LIFE.

Make your own light. Don't wait for the one at the end of the tunnel. Make your own hope. Remember the moments. Hold onto the joy. The MAGIC, the MEMORIES, the LIGHT is yours.

The memory of love has bound us together in a circle of FAMILY and together we shall light up the world.

IF I COULD JUST SEE HOPE…I CAN…RIGHT HERE…INSIDE WHERE LOVE AND MEMORY ARE FOREVER IN MY HEART. IF I COULD SEE HOPE — IT'S THE MAGIC AND THE MEMORY OF YOU.